HIGHWAYS OF PROGRESS

CHAPTER V

COMMERCE

COMMERCE is the exchange of commodities, and the term is generally understood to include the buying and selling between individuals and, in a wider sense, between communities and nations. Under its adventurous leadership civilization and Christianity have spread to the remotest parts of the world. The commercial nations have, at all times exercised the strongest influence for good among the peoples of the earth.

The development of commerce is the effort by a country to find a market for its own productions or to supply its own necessities or to increase further its means of commercial expansion. The commercial expansion of a nation is the index of its growth. This commercial growth may be either domestic or foreign, or both.

There are three books which, if accurately written, would be found to follow parallel lines, dealing with the same material and proceeding from the same starting place to the same goal; these are the History of Commerce, the History of Transportation and the History of Civilization. So intimately related to every step of man's progress is this interchange of commodities, drawing along with it the interchange of ideas and the selection of those best fitted to advance the world!

Commerce, as an agent in modern life, has been sometimes unduly exalted and sometimes unfairly abused. It is neither the sole purpose of national life nor is it in any way necessarily connected with public or private impropriety. The word "commercialism" may cover the noblest as well as the basest things. But from the beginning of human intercourse, the barter of the savage which taught him that there were people, ideas, interests, capacities separate from his own, and thus applied a rude intellectual stimulus, down to the present time when international traffic has made of the whole world one huge place of exchange, commerce has been the softener of differences, the teacher of the undeveloped man, the emissary of new customs, new standards, better ways and larger thoughts — the effectual servant of the common human life.

An occupation so ancient and universal, so knit to other industry wherever man has emerged from barbarism, and so growing with his growth, scarcely requires distinct treatment in a survey of any national development. It becomes rather a general measure of progress; and in one form or another the discussion of it enters into every chapter of a nation's history.

More and more, with the increase in number and efficiency of methods of communication, commerce has become a world affair. Until a comparatively short time ago it was specialized and limited. The

China trade, the India trade, the Guinea trade, the trade of Venice and Spain and Portugal and Holland down to the end of the eighteenth century were distinct and independent commercial ventures, more or less perfectly controlled and jealously guarded. Now, with only such limitations as tariffs impose and such regulations as hamper the carrying trade, the people of any part of the globe may and do trade with the people of any other part with no feeling of strangeness. The earth is becoming, commercially, one big exchange; in which, however, the principal traders are still those nations which race instinct or the habit of centuries has accustomed to the carrying on of commercial interchanges. Preconceived notions on this point have to be laid aside.

First, the genius for commerce does not depend upon what we call civilization. It may be developed by the crowding of population, the necessity of finding new occupations, the need of realizing in some way upon a country's surplus product, whatever that may be. In some cases the instinct for trade appears to be an inheritance. It has been the property of the peoples of the Far East, in many respects so unlike us moderns, for centuries. And one of the most interesting features of their awakening is the fact that this quality of theirs grows more rapidly and vigorously than almost any other in the new atmosphere. The way in which the nations of the Orient are pushing their commercial affairs is worthy of our attention and emulation. We may call them uncivilized, but they are not. We may think that we shall build up a great trade with them, but we must remember that they are as quick at trading as we. The "Yankee" as a dealer may meet more than his match at Yokohama or Hongkong.

Second, the mere existence of a market shows an opportunity; nothing more. It may not be an opportunity for us, or we may not have the intelligence or the energy or the facilities required to take full advantage of it. Japan cannot feed her own people. They would buy very largely from us if we could only sell to them. China spends vast sums for iron and steel, yet we furnish only a small quantity of it, while the big percentage goes to England and Germany. These people, with a low cost of living and a low wage scale, cannot pay our prices. Every step in their growth, numbering as they do from four hundred millions to half a billion, reaching out daily for means to develop their resources — for all the thousand aids that other countries further advanced in industrial methods can supply — marks a big commercial possibility. Yet our trade with the Orient is almost moribund. We cannot create a great commerce with any people who cannot sell advantageously in our market as well as buy. We cannot trade largely with a country if we cannot compete with others in its markets.

Third, the expansion of our foreign market is not in proportion to our internal growth and resources. Because the total of our foreign trade increases annually, we are encouraged to boast of it. It grows mostly because it has to; because it would be a miracle if it did not, when population and every form of domestic industry show an increase so great. But glance at some comparative figures.

The combined imports and exports of this country in 1906 were $2,970,426,946; in 1907, $3,315,272,503; in 1908, $3,055,115,138; and in 1909, $2,974,931,328. Thus our entire foreign trade increased $344,845,557 in 1907 over 1906. Between 1907 and 1908 it decreased $260,157,365. The net increase for the three years is $4,500,000. Our exports alone increased between 1906 and 1907 by $136,986,578, and decreased between 1907 and 1909 by $217,839,974. What was happening meantime to our real wealth, the backbone of our commerce? The value of farm products increased $360,000,000 between 1907 and 1908, and $1,023,000,000 in the two years between 1906 and 1908.

Comparisons with other nations in fields where we should have an advantage over them are equally significant. Except Canada, whose business is bound up with ours by ties of nature and by great railroad and water systems, there is no country whose trade we should control so certainly as Mexico. It is at our doors, it is a republic, its relations with us are friendly and large amounts of American capital have been invested there. Mexico is growing rapidly. Who gets the benefit? The large gains in the foreign trade of that country for 1907 as compared with 1906 were apportioned as follows: Germany, $1,872,739; Great Britain, $1,698,867; France, $728,307; United States, $415,806. Our total trade with Mexico fell off by more than $21,000,000 in 1908 as compared with 1907. In 1909 it decreased by nearly $5,000,000 more.

Take another country where we should have a distinct advantage. Argentina is a big field, expanding yearly, and we need no Panama Canal to reach her. Her trade might be mostly with our country. Here is a record of the increase or decrease of her foreign commerce, distributed by countries, for the first six months of 1907 as compared with the same period in 1906:

	IMPORTS FROM	EXPORTS TO
Germany	+$3,275,325	+ $198,480
Belgium	+ 1,968,993	+4,132,071
France	— 407,559	+ 3,506,876
United Kingdom . .	+ 8,567,677	— 615,457
United States . . .	— 966,129	—1,283,434

The increase in importations into Argentina for the first quarter of 1908, as compared with the same period in 1907, was distributed as follows: United States, $186,690; United Kingdom, $5,873,021; Germany, $3,393,224; Italy, $2,747,934; France, $1,147,242. Such statistics tell their own story, and they might be continued indefinitely.

Fourth, it is the nations north of the equator who are gifted with a genius for commerce and the resources that diversify and enrich it. Less than six per cent. of the population of the globe lies south of the equator, and this includes a large proportion of non-commercial races. North of that line the great commercial development of the last two centuries has taken place. It has been hastened by competition and the march of useful invention. It has been retarded by the long war of edicts against trade, hostile tariffs, reprisals, and all that human ingenuity enlisted in the aid of selfishness could do to repress its growth or divert it into channels other than those indicated by nature. None of the great physical laws which have helped upward the races that came to know and work with them can take precedence of the laws that govern commerce, and work themselves out to ends universally beneficent in spite of the little attempts of men and nations to turn them from their course or to alter their purpose; which is the amalgamating of human societies and the diffusion of all the good things earth has to offer among all earth's children.

The question of commerce is, fundamentally, a question of markets. The main commercial needs of every people advanced beyond the primitive stage are two; an adequate market in which their products may be sold at a fair price, and an opportunity to purchase on reasonable terms those things which they cannot supply for themselves. Domestic commerce in this country is incomparably more important than foreign. We have no accurate measure of its volume, but it exceeds all our transactions in the outside field put together many fold. The foreign market assumes prominence in the public mind because it is there that our surplus must be disposed of. How small our business with South America is has already been shown by one example. We do from ten to eleven per cent. of that trade. With Canada we do better; and, were there reasonable liberty for commerce to develop, free from the restraint of obstructive tariffs, this might eventually become our best customer. In the Orient, as elsewhere shown, we might find buyers for our surplus cotton and food staples, as long as we have any surplus to dispose of, and our steel manufactures, at least until its own resources are developed. But restraints upon trade, not created by corporations but forged by legislative action, have almost forced the discontinuance of successful and promising efforts to find an outlet there. With the increase of our population, this problem of markets is one of those that the future will have to solve.

A market without means of communication between buyer and seller is like a meal placed out of reach of the hungry man. In our big market, which will always be the United States itself, the railroads are the factors that determine success or failure. In the chapters on "The Railroad," their function will be examined more in detail; and in that on "Waterways" is discussed the aid that may naturally be expected from our navigable streams in the conduct of domestic trade. It is remarkable, however, in any survey of natural conditions, to find that most public activity has been devoted to checking and embarrassing the interest without which the bulk of our internal and substantially all our foreign trade would perish in a fortnight. We are, indeed, pledged to spend a sum, which no one any longer dares to estimate even within a margin of a hundred millions, on the construction of the Panama

Canal. It will, no doubt, have its uses, especially for the southern portion of this country. But it does not lie in the highway of our foreign commerce, and it opens to us no markets save those which we have already failed to improve.

A real care for foreign trade requires the larger view. The world is bound together so closely by the ties of commerce that nothing can be high or scarce for any length of time if there is a supply anywhere on the face of the earth. Ships or rails will find it and bring it to market. We used to think of the travels of Mungo Park as something remarkable; but not now. Darkest Africa is almost a matter of daily information. And with this fusing of the world by commerce into virtually one community, the race will be to the intelligent, the enterprising, to those who can supply the best articles in the shortest time at the lowest prices. That is the final word of the modern commercial system.

What do we need to achieve the success that ought to come to a people like ours, furnished with resources such as no others possess? As far as commerce with other countries is concerned, we have to realize that we can no more fight the battles of trade with the policies of a century ago than we could carry a war through successfully if our soldiers were armed with blunderbusses, which they had to load from powder horn and bullet pouch. The modern system of maximum and minimum tariffs has decided that no one country can profit long at the expense of discrimination

against others. The United States has been behind
a stone wall. It was a pretty good defence against
arrows, but it will not withstand the artillery of the
commercial systems of to-day; and it is worth nothing
when you have to sally out from behind it and meet
your competitors in the open field. We make low
freight rates on commodities for export to our seaports,
and there meet regulations that prevent us from
competing. We build up some trade on the basis of
overcharging the home consumer to pay for selling
cheap to the foreign customer; and no such system
can be permanent. We place an embargo on enterprise. We can enjoy the home market as a monopoly,
and make what there is in it, or we can go out and take
our place in the markets of the world and join in the
world struggle for that business. But we cannot
do both at the same time; and the sooner this is realized,
the better it will be for the country.

We need for our trade and for every agency connected with it a larger measure of the freedom that
our government guarantees to the individual as a
citizen. We need encouragement for those who are
seeking and making new markets in the remote
places of the earth; and such necessary and proper
assistance for our merchant marine, for the agencies
actually engaged in commerce, the transporters of
products, and not swift passenger and mail lines,
as will put us on an equality in the carrying trade with
the other commercial nations. Before we can compete
with them at all. of course there must be an abolition

of the rule requiring publication of foreign rates before they can be changed; a condition now imposed by law, which enables any tramp steamship to underbid any American carrier in any port of the world. It is equivalent to the forced transfer by law of the business of American ships to those under any flag which see fit to cut a rate in order to get business away from their competitors.

Most crying of all, perhaps, is the need for more information among our politicians. They propose and carry through restrictions upon commerce like that just referred to, of whose effect some are profoundly ignorant, while some are actuated by demagogy and malice. Men who are mere demagogues, and other men who mean well but do not know, have never made a study of commerce, join hands to put into effect legislation that is mischievous in principle and can be only injurious in operation. Objection, criticism, even pleas for delay until there may be full consideration, advanced by experienced men, are ascribed to unworthy motives. Many men of high ability and unblemished character in the United States Senate have been attacked and have actually fallen into some popular disrepute because they opposed ill-considered legislation which the study and experience of a lifetime had told them could work out only in misfortune to commercial interests and all the people dependent upon them. A recent critic of our institutions has said that the provisions of our Constitution and the difficulty of changing them render our

Government less responsive to changing ideas than those of more conservative peoples, living under systems far less liberal in their beginning and history. The remark would be more applicable to our commercial system, and the archaic or meddlesome legislation that underlies much of it. The people of the American Colonies had no greater need of a Declaration of Independence than the people of the United States have of an act of emancipation which shall free commerce from the fetters, old and new, that now impede every movement toward her rightful and possible triumph.

A free, prosperous and intelligent people, with a high standard of living and the still higher standard of efficiency that should exist in such an environment, and that must be established and maintained if we are to do anything worth while in the world, will create the greatest and most profitable commerce, will occupy to most advantage both the home and the foreign fields when troubled by fewest conditions and regulations. Because commerce has to do with commodities gathered or manufactured by the hand of man, and is carried on with means of communication created or improved by men, governments and individuals find it difficult to understand that it is, nevertheless, subject to inherent natural laws just as irresistible and as proof against man's efforts to alter them as any of the great natural processes observed in the rise of human society. Cheap little victories won by artificial devices, transient and accidental advantage, all are worthless. A survey of the resources and development of the United States shows that her supremacy in commerce should be as unquestioned as her superiority in natural wealth, the native ability of her people and her system of transportation. But with reference to no other interest is there need of a closer study of laws and conditions; of policies based upon scientific principles rather than popular clamour; of a wise union of liberty with regulation, and encouragement to and reliance upon the natural forces that have directed the intercourse of other people for thousands of years and will guide it to the end.

CHAPTER VI

INDUSTRIAL AND RAILROAD CONSOLIDATIONS

ALL progress is the development of order. A uniform method is the highest form of order. The benefit accruing to a people and their progress will be in proportion to the extent of their application of uniform methods to the production of what they require. This is the general law which may be discerned behind recent changes of method in the industrial world, too often foolishly attributed to some deliberate and evil plan of masterful individuals or large aggregations of capital. These are but instruments in the working out of the law; and it is of sufficient scope and importance, not only in our national life but in the world's life, to merit a more patient and impartial study than it usually receives.

The tendency toward combination of interests engaged in large industrial undertakings is simply a part of that cooperation in the production, the distribution and the exchange of wealth with which everybody has been familiar for centuries. When the pioneers in this country united to help build one another's houses, when they had a barn "raising," it was combination. When the owner of land or implements or capital in any other form first entered into partnership with labour to create more wealth, it was combination. When the corporation came into existence, through which many small amounts of capital could be massed, it marked a new era, just as much as when two men first lifted by their united strength some stone or tree trunk too heavy for them singly. Exactly as society and the work of the community have become more complex, so have the means by which material ends are achieved grown larger and more powerful. The union of numerous disconnected and weak railroads in one orderly and efficient system, the substitution of one great establishment for many small plants, are part of the natural and inevitable evolution of united action among men.

One misconception needs to be removed at the outset, in considering combinations of capital. I know no theory so fallacious as the popular conception of the nature and purpose of the consolidation of wealth. It does not mean the hoarding of money in a bag, so that its one possessor may delve in it up to his armpits. It means rather the effective organization of effort, the intelligent use of money which represents exerted physical or mental energy. The common conception of the capitalist as a man who hoards money, and of Wall Street as a place where the money supply of the country may be cornered and kept, to be doled out to the people only as they submit to terms imposed by its owners, no more represents any existing reality than does the picture of a dragon. For few things are more worthless or uneasy than capital unemployed;

and wealth locked up in vaults in a great city is just as useless to its possessor as heaps of gold to Robinson Crusoe. Idle capital may create a national problem, and has caused widespread national distress, as surely as idle labour.

The people who propose to sweep the new business method out of existence as a public menace forget one thing. We have reached a stage of national development where business must be done on a different plan from that which served half a century ago. In 1865 we had thirty-five millions of people. To-day we have nearly ninety millions. By the middle of the century we shall have two hundred millions. Less than thirty-five years ago horse cars filled the needs of urban transportation. To-day we could not possibly get along without the trolley. In economic conditions, as in physical conditions, we must keep pace with the times. If the masses of the people are to continue to enjoy the prosperity and the comforts which they desire, old-fashioned methods are inadequate. People in this country live better to-day than they ever did before. They are better fed, housed and clothed. There are fewer drones in the hive, fewer people who share the results of work without working themselves, less waste in the necessary processes by which population is sustained and business conducted.

These are consequences of the better organization of industry, of which large combinations are an important feature. It is as useless to propose doing without them as it would be to go back to the horse car, or to insist that the shoemaker at his bench should make with his hands the entire amount of footwear used by all the people of the country. And this expansion and improvement of method must continue. It will not move backward.

There has been and still is a more or less common feeling of hostility on the part of the public toward consolidations, though it is yielding perceptibly to the growth of intelligence and to the demonstration of benefits in many instances by the conduct of industry on a large scale. This attitude is pronounced, but the reasons for it are not always plainly stated. Some of it is due to the unfortunate form taken by combination at the beginning in this country. To obviate ruinous competition, what were called "trusts" were formed. Under this system the stocks of various and competing organizations were trusteed in the hands of a few men, to whom was given arbitrary authority to do as they pleased with the properties under their control. This was not a wholesome arrangement. It was a cumbrous structure, and it was declared illegal by the courts. It exists now, if at all, secretly, and must not be confounded with the rise of one big company out of many small ones, which is the feature of industrial consolidation. But it lasted long enough to stir up prejudice that has been transferred to some extent to a successor altogether different.

Most opposition, however, is based upon the proposition that the so-called "trusts" — for we still lack in common usage a more fitting name for industrial combinations — work toward monopoly. The monopolistic feature, with its supposed control of product and command of prices, fills the public mind to such an extent that the underlying principle has been too little considered.

On this point several facts contrary to the extreme monopolistic theory may be noted:

First: The largest manufacturing combination in this country does not control 50 per cent. of the product of the commodity it deals with.

Second: Unrestricted competition has shown itself no unmixed blessing. In many cases it has produced results as evil as those of complete monopoly would be if such a thing existed.

Third: No combination in this country will ever rise superior to public opinion or be able long to defy it. Virtual monopolies that control through price agreements certain lines of manufactured articles would be smashed by the abolition of protective duties on these articles. An actual monopoly, controlling all production and squeezing the people, could and would be driven out of business by popular revolt.

Fourth: Steadiness of prices and profits is regarded by capital everywhere, and by every management intelligent enough to hold its place, as far more desirable than excessive prices and undue profits.

Fifth: It thus appears that there is a law of balance and proportion in the operation of consolidated industries, not at first perceived or known, which insists upon moderation as a condition of their very existence and will destroy them, sooner or later, if violated.

Sixth: There is the regulative power of actual law, exhibited in "anti-trust" statutes all over the country, which at present tends rather to bind industrial development harmfully than allow to it dangerous freedom. Undoubtedly, if consolidation should ever threaten the public welfare or the place of the individual as a free industrial unit, this authority would be further asserted and extended.

These are all valid reasons why the popular antipathy to all forms of combination should be laid aside, and the subject investigated without prepossession, like any other phenomenon, such as different systems of land tenure, or the value of synthetic chemistry in manufacture, or other changes in industrial method within very recent times.

Assuming the public to be able to protect itself against extortion, there are only a few men in the community who can advance good reasons for opposition to the new system. These are the middlemen, and the small competitor who is unable to meet the larger concern in open market. They are caught between the upper and the nether millstones. The former has no just reason for complaint. He is not a producer. His work was just so much economic waste, which is saved by shortening the connection between producer and consumer. The latter is less freely forced to the wall than is supposed.

It has appeared in nearly all the investigations

recently conducted under the Sherman anti-trust law that the small competitor still exists; that as soon as he is forced out or bought out, another of him appears; that no pressure is strong enough to eliminate him altogether, and that the wisest concerns neither try nor desire to do so. But, in so far as the small business man is put at a disadvantage, we must consider his injury, if the principle of consolidation has come to stay, as only one more instance of the hardships that always accompany progress.

So far as we can see now, the greatest number — whose good must be considered first — is benefited, just as it has been by the invention of machinery. Yet every machine displaces many men. The printer who set type by hand has had to find another job since the linotype came into general use. Almost every improvement that helps the many brings injury to individuals here and there. The building of a railroad puts the owner of the stage coach out of business. All the trades have been revolutionized by machinery that threw men out of work or forced them to learn a new trade. But the community gains by the cheapening of processes and of prices, so that the balance is in favour of the improvements. We are so alive to the blessings of progress that we are apt to forget that they always cost something. But the advantage is great and sure, and the world has never refused to grasp it and pay the necessary price.

On the other side of the balance sheet we may see what this compensating advantage is. In every such industrial improvement the chief beneficiary is the working man. For his gain is double; one in wages, and another in cheaper and more abundant food, shelter and clothing. By combining several concerns in one, many economies are made possible. Useless officers and unproductive middlemen are cut off. The systems of purchase and distribution are simplified. Economies are effected by the direct purchase of material in large quantities, or, better still, by acquisition of ample supplies of raw material. This enables the United States Steel Corporation to make high profits on its immense capitalization, at prices which give to smaller concerns only a modest return.

The utilization of waste products is another economy which now not unfrequently furnishes the entire dividends of important factories; and when this has been carried as far and with as careful direction by practical chemists in the United States as in Germany, the results will be still more marked. The Carnegie Company built up its great success upon the fact that it took its iron from its own mines, made its coke in its own ovens, worked up its material in its own furnaces and shipped the finished product over its own railroad or in its own vessels. In the great Krupp Iron Works, of Germany, this system has been in operation for two generations; and, instead of arousing public antagonism, the Krupps have the admiration and good-will of the entire German nation from the Emperor down.

Now this system obviously enables capital and labour to produce a better article at a lower first cost; and that is the rule of industrial progress in this country. Sometimes the demand for cheapness is too pressing, and quality deteriorates; but this quickly rights itself. Sometimes prices are forced up, but there is always in reserve capital and enterprise enough to enter the field when these pass the boundary of a reasonable profit.

It is a common habit to attribute the rise of prices during the last ten years entirely to combinations and resulting monopoly. In some instances these have contributed, but there are other powerful causes. The increase in wages and the decrease in hours of labour, the protective tariff that excludes foreign competition, and the enormous increase in the volume of money and credits might account for the whole of the increase in prices. So far as modern industrial methods are concerned, we may fairly say that their net result has been to cheapen production, and thus to place more of the comforts of life within the reach of the people.

That the condition of labour has been improved by the growth of big employing concerns is patent. Strikes are more infrequent when a general schedule of wages is fixed by a central management. This can be done when the danger of disturbance to trade through erratic action by some individual operator is lessened. It is easier for organized labour to deal with organized capital. Within the last ten years it has been shown repeatedly how much more infrequent are ruptures between large corporations and their employees, and how much more prompt and satisfactory the settlement than when disturbance might arise in any one of a score of centers and be prolonged through the obstinacy of any one of a score of managements or labour committees. The big concern can afford to purchase and must have the latest and most improved machinery. It cannot afford to lay off its men except in extreme cases, because the loss of a day is a serious item in its business.

The workingmen, too, may participate in profits by investing their savings in the shares of the more solid and prosperous concerns. The profits of the old corporation went to a very few persons. It is easy for even a labourer to know in these days what consolidations are organized and run on a business basis, and he has such an opportunity as never before for safe and lucrative investment that will enable him to share in the gains of his own labour and his employer's capital. Of the nearly $4,000,000,000 of deposits in the savings banks of this country, the bulk consists of the savings of labour; and this represents but a portion of its accumulations. With such resources, the workingmen of the country might, if they chose, practically control a large part of its industry within a few years. From every point of view, the workingman, representing the greatest number whose good a sound industrial order must seek, appears to be the principal gainer from the new order in the world of wealth production.

We must beware, however, of rash and sweeping conclusions in either direction. One of the great faults of the American public is its readiness to accept extreme views. The system of combination in business has been denounced in unmeasured terms. We have seen that it does not deserve such abuse. Neither, probably, is it the universal panacea that many people think it, or destined to be final in its present shape. We are, as yet, no more than on the threshold of the new era. We must draw proper distinctions.

Already it is clear enough that the greatest value of industrial combination lies in the fields calling for immense capital, where big quantities of raw material must be controlled, huge plants erected, costly machinery provided and a universal demand supplied. The big instrument is for the big work, such as the iron and steel trade and its like. In some lines the old-fashioned small corporations will do the work better, and they are doing it. A railroad does not use the same locomotive for its mountain division and its switching yards.

The theory that business consolidation in certain employments is a good policy for everybody appears to be justified by experience. Against the alleged injury that is intangible can be set the benefit which figures prove — benefit to the workingman, to the consumer, to the capitalist. Wages are higher, prices have not risen in proportion, well-chosen investments are safer, more productive and more certain of return. The unsound combination must be weeded out; and time is doing that. The proper boundaries within which consolidation is the best working principle must be ascertained; and time and experience are doing that. When a longer trial has taught us more of the new method, and removed or restrained its abuses, it will undoubtedly be discovered that much has been added by it to the resources, the productive power and the well-being of man as an individual worker, and still more to the efficiency of the industrial association of mankind.

Fiercer than the controversy over the relative merits of competition and consolidation as applied to manufacture has been the discussion of them as applied to transportation. Originally the railroad property of the country consisted of a large number of small pieces of track, operated by companies unconnected with and often hostile to one another. This was natural in a period when the main purpose of the railroad was still to serve local needs; to connect with the larger business centres of the country the territory immediately served by them.

With the settlement of the West, and especially with the growth of through traffic, a new condition arose. The difficulty of sending commodities over half a dozen lines, operated by as many companies, in one quick and continuous journey became too great for business to bear. What happened to the currency of the country happened to its railroad business. In the period before the war it was possible for the people to get along with notes issued by state banks because business was largely local, travel was limited and financial enterprises comparatively small. Such a system would be intolerable to-day. And to handle the immense through railroad business of this country by a host of small and isolated lines would be just as impracticable as to carry on our commerce with forty-six different kinds of money. Consolidation appeared as naturally and as inevitably as the triple expansion engine displaces that of an earlier type.

Now this was an economic evolution, independent of the plans or wishes of men. It had to be, just as men had to learn the use of fire if they were to become civilized. But a vast pother rose over the change; a cloud of law-making appeared; the comparative desirability of free competition and general consolidation in the transportation business was debated with a sort of frenzy, as if it could be settled by words; and men are still talking and legislative bodies still passing new laws to establish or save competition in railroading, as if this were something under their control. The building of parallel lines has been encouraged and bitter rate wars have been welcomed as an assurance to the people of competition for their benefit.

As a matter of fact, these things mean the waste of capital supplied by the people; mean losses paid by the people. If there are two lines where one would suffice, the added burden falls on the public. A railroad must either earn money to operate it, or borrow. In either case the people foot the bills. The fortunes of railroad companies are determined by the law of the survival of the fittest. This has already grouped the railroads of other countries into a few great systems, operated in harmony with one another. It has reduced scores of railroad corporations in New England to two systems, whose merger is substantially accomplished. All over the country it has built up big, efficient transportation machines, out of little scraps of lines that served neither the public nor their stockholders satisfactorily. And the interesting fact, as we shall see in the later chapters devoted to "The Railroad" specifically, is that this process has been contemporaneous with such a cheapening of the cost of transportation to the public as was never known before in the history of the world, and with a re- markable development of efficiency in the handling of an unprecedented volume of business.

The law-making authority has fluttered about this natural and necessary transformation much as a fly buzzes about a horse. It can sting and annoy, but it neither hastens nor impedes the progress of the horse un- less the flies are thick enough and can bite hard enough to bring him to a halt in the effort to drive them away.

In the first place, railroad consolidation was pro- hibited by law almost everywhere, because it was considered destructive of competition. Now, whatever may be argued about competition in the abstract, it can apply to transportation only in the large field and the large sense. To a certain extent, a railroad is a natural monopoly. There is room for only so many in a given territory. Excessive competition may encour- age temporary rate cutting; but no business can ever continue long on a losing basis. Sooner or later a restoration of rates, some understanding or agreement,

comes to make existence possible to the railroads;
and then for every line in the territory in excess of
what is required to carry its business, the public will
pay and continue to pay. Self-preservation, which
is a law stronger than any legislature, has nullified
competition over large areas, manifestly to the welfare
of their people. Consolidation still proceeds, and the
impossibility of arresting it or doing the business of
the country without it is now admitted even by those
who would protest against removing these inoperative
laws from the statute book.

It also happened, curiously enough, that while
legislative bodies were forbidding consolidation through
one set of laws, they were compelling it through another.
The assertion by the state of control of the rate-making
power, in the slightest degree, at once logically destroyed
the possibility of competition. For universal competition can exist only where prices are absolutely free
to go up and down without regulation or limit; until
the competing concerns and the public that they serve
meet on the level of the cheapest service that is consistent with a reasonable profit, or until some competitors
are forced to the wall. Competition involves and
requires charges which are at times unreasonable,
unequal and unfair. It thrives on discrimination.
From the moment when these things were banned by
the law, combination was authorized and forced.

The principles of rate-making laid down in the
interstate commerce law and the decisions rendered
under it absolutely prohibit competition. Ever since

they became effective, railroads have been obliged to come together, to agree on rates over large areas, to save expense by making one management do what it had taken many to do before. As has been shown, permanent competition in railroading would be impossible in the nature of things. But the force which has hastened consolidation and imposed it upon all railroads that would render good service at a fair price and also keep out of bankruptcy is the rate regulation of the last twenty-five years. To this end the wholly contradictory ideas of law-makers, supporting competition, opposing combination, and yet ordering uniformity of rates under heavy penalties, have worked together until the public itself has accepted the modern method as a necessity. It will presently recognize it as a good.

For, in addition to the benefits pointed out as consequences of consolidation in industrial growth, especially as affecting the workingman, many others have accrued to the public by reason of the grouping of railroads into large systems. In Europe, where the population is dense, this fact has long been recognized, and the paralleling of a railroad is forbidden by law. Good service can be given only by a road that is making money. The people are the chief sufferers wherever a railroad is operated at a loss. Formerly every small railroad that began nowhere and ended at the crossroads had its president, vice-president and full complement of other officers, all drawing good salaries. For these there is now one series of officers and one set of salaries. Economy has marked every stage of the welding of these little railroads together; but all other gains are insignificant when compared with the enormous increase of efficiency in operation and the decrease in cost to the public.

I will not go into this matter here at length, since I shall discuss it fully and with the necessary statistical comparisons in other chapters, and give a measure of the practical transformation of the transportation business by consolidation; of how, by this means alone, the carriers of the country have been enabled to handle its business and, at the same time, reduce rates until the freight charges on American railroads are only a fraction of those in other countries.

The whole story can be compressed into a single statement. The last twenty-five years cover the period of active consolidation among the railroads of the United States, until the extent of the groups that will finally survive and the territory served by each can be roughly approximated. While this was going on, the average receipt per passenger per mile on all the railroads of the United States dropped from 2.42 cents in 1883 to 2.01 cents in 1906; and the average freight rate per ton per mile fell nearly 40 per cent., from 1.22 cents to .77.

In fact, every legitimate railroad combination, by which I mean one having a business as distinguished from a stock-jobbing motive, is intended to produce and does produce better service and lower rates on the side of the public, and either larger or more certain profits or both on the side of the stockholder.

Take the Northern Securities Company for example. It contemplated no power and had no power under its charter to operate a railroad. The purpose of it was to enable owners of large amounts of stock in both the Great Northern and the Northern Pacific companies to put them into a common holding concern, where they would be secure against change. It was a labour-saving device, and a device contributing to the welfare of the public by assuring in the management of great properties that security, harmony and relief from various forms of waste out of which grow lower rates just as surely as dividends. The courts asserted that it had the power to restrain trade; that the power to do a thing is as objectionable as the doing of it; that is to say, that since with your hand you may kill a man, it is against public policy for a man to have hands.

So the Northern Securities Company went out of business. What has been the result? What is the difference? To the owners of the properties, merely the inconvenience of holding two certificates of stock of different colours instead of one, and of keeping track of two different sets of securities. To the public, no difference at all except that it has missed the advantages which the simpler and more businesslike plan would have secured.

Take the purchase of the Burlington property by the Great Northern and the Northern Pacific jointly. What was the purpose and what the results of that? The public seems to think that when a consolidation of properties is effected, all the small stockholders will, by some mysterious and awful process, be "frozen out," and that their property will be gobbled up by a few men. Nobody has lost anything by this transaction. The Burlington reaches over its own rails Chicago, Peoria, Rock Island, Davenport, St. Louis, St. Joseph, Kansas City, Omaha, Denver, and thus connects with the main arteries of traffic of the whole country. All the large slaughter houses of the country are located in centres reached by that road. Four-fifths of the silver and lead smelters in the United States are situated along it. In counties reached by the Burlington system in Illinois, 90 per cent. of the manufacturing in the state is done. Much of its territory offers a market for the lumber of the Pacific Coast. To put these markets and products in touch with one another is worth something.

If hundreds of millions of dollars had been raised to construct this system, or if another like it had been built beside it with new capital, it would have been hailed everywhere with approval as a means of bringing the Northwest and the Southwest together, of increasing the business of all the lines concerned and adding to the prosperity of both sections of the country. This is what has been brought about without the waste of capital involved in duplicating construction; and the service is just as real, the benefit just as susceptible of proof.

The question of stock ownership is to be considered in the light of a great competitive condition between the territories served by different large systems. There is competition between the Northwest and the Southwest. There is effort to develop each section of the country, to secure business for and from one as against another. This form of competition has not been destroyed, and it is probably the only kind that is destined to remain fully operative in the transportation business. Consolidation is merely an incident on the road to efficient service. It cannot be against public interest, for we have already seen the greatest decline of rates in the period when it was proceeding most rapidly. It threatens no other dangers, because railway companies are subject to supervision and control, now extended to almost every detail of their operation, by the public. The amount of their capital is public. Their rates must be public and uniform. Reasonableness of rates and service does not depend upon whether one man owns the capital stock of a railway or whether it is held by ten or ten thousand; by persons or corporations. And the courts are always open to see that the obligations of the common carrier are performed.

The public, on its part, must understand that it cannot afford to build up a commercial system based on the supposition that the transportation business will be done at a loss. No such arrangement can possibly be permanent. Railroad rates and regulations, when prescribed by public authority, may easily be made such that no financial return for service remains after paying expenses. Somewhere before this point is reached the line must be drawn. Otherwise, if hope of a fair profit is cut off, private capital will no longer be put into railroads. Such conditions have been known in this country recently, and might easily become fixed. Then, since the traffic of the country must be carried, the only recourse would be to have the Government do the work. We can know what this would certainly mean.

The experience of state-owned railroads in Europe, in Mexico and elsewhere, unable to sustain themselves without rates much higher than ours, although labour is far cheaper, our own experience in the conduct of all large undertakings by the government, proves that the work would cost from 50 per cent. more to several times as much as now. This added cost, together with the disadvantages of an inferior service, would fall on the people. They would have to carry the burden forever. They should take a second serious thought before inviting this possibility by measures so drastic and unfair that capital will no longer engage in railroad enterprises.

Whatever, then, may be thought of the application of the principle of combination to manufacturing, its work in connection with transportation appears to have been as beneficent as we have learned all natural laws to be when we have ceased to fear and begun to understand them. It is introducing system into the railroad business of the country. It is cutting out waste, driving out speculative interests, organizing transportation in a national sense as has never been done before, to the advantage of everybody concerned.

For in the end the only community of interests that can exist permanently is the community between the producer of tonnage and the carrier. The railroads depend for their existence upon the products of the land they serve. The man out on the farm or in the forest or down in the mine must be able to sell his product at a profit, or he will cease to labour. When he has nothing to sell, there will be nothing for the railroad to carry. Individuals come and go, but the land of the country, its resources and the railroads will be here permanently; and they will either prosper or be poor together.

There is one plain evil connected with the creation of certain great corporations that has not been corrected, although it is easily reached. The valid objection to many concerns, especially some of those known as "industrials," is that they appear to have been created in the first place not so much for the purpose of manufacturing any particular commodity as for selling sheaves of printed securities which represent nothing more than the good will and prospective profits of the promoters. Nearly all the large concerns engaged in manufacture or trade that have come to grief owe their downfall to excessive capitalization. This is a real menace not only to their successful existence but to the public, which pays prices based to some extent on the desire to make profits on more than the money invested.

If it is the will of the general Government to prevent the growth of such corporations, it has always seemed to me that a simple remedy was within its reach. Under the constitutional provision allowing Congress to regulate commerce between the states, any company desiring to transact business outside of the state in which it is incorporated should be held to a uniform provision of Federal law; namely, that all should satisfy a commission that their capital stock was actually paid up in cash or in property taken at a fair valuation, just as the capital of a national bank must be certified to be paid up by the controller of the currency.

It is only fair to a dealer in Minnesota or California or Oregon that, if a company claims to have ten, twenty, or fifty millions of capital, and wishes to do business in that state, he should know that its solvency and the honesty of its alleged capitalization have been passed upon by a Federal commission. With such a simple provision of law, the temptation to make companies for the purpose of selling prospective profits would be at an end; and, at the same time, no legitimate business would suffer. Nor could any number of individuals desirous of engaging in business as a corporation suffer any hardship by being obliged to prove that their capital was as advertised; that they were not beginning to deal with the public under false pretenses.

I am convinced that this is the simplest, most effective and necessary regulation to be applied to modern business methods. It begins at the beginning. It not only attacks the practice by which millions of the people's money have been coaxed into bad investments, but it also bears directly upon the main evil attributed to the existence of big corporations. With it they would lose most of their incentive to any such wrong-doing as may be within their power. With it there would be little inducement to claim exorbitant profits by raising prices, because the fact could no longer be concealed by spreading the net return over a fictitious capitalization.

And of course it follows equally that where capital has been fully paid in, no interference should be allowed, because no injustice would be likely to be done. Yet, although this remedy has been all the time within easy reach, although it has been before the public, I myself calling attention to and recommending it in an address and in published articles eight years ago, it is still untried, while legislators go on debating the impossible suppression of a natural law.

The laws of trade are as certain in their operation as the laws of gravitation. The combination of forces to accomplish ends to which singly they are unequal is one of these natural laws. You might as well try to set a broken arm by statute as to change a commercial law by legislative enactment. We have been as a nation too ready to look to State and Federal legislation for remedies beyond their power to give. You may obstruct and delay for a time, but in the end the inex-orable law of experience and the survival of the fittest will prevail. That is a law of universal operation, and in its working it appears to be eternal. The wise course for us is to try all things, to keep that which is good, to work with intelligence and by the light of past experience toward that which is better, and thus to sift methods and secure in the end results beneficial to every individual, to every interest, to national development and prosperity.

Such combinations as are evil, and some there are, will be found self-destroying. The large material view of things as well as the moral shows that the affairs of men are subject to a moral order. That which is wrong cannot continue indefinitely. Every mistake carries within it the seed of failure. Every device of man is tried by final facts; and not one which is not fitted to promote his progress and to assist in the betterment of human conditions and the advance of human societies will survive. All history shows this. Therefore, in so far as the principle of collective effort through great corporations is wholly self-seeking, aims at unjust ends or offends the law of national growth, it will perish.

Especially in a country of free institutions and among a people accustomed to act independently it is impossible to conceive of any lasting triumph of a bad method. The people of this country could to-morrow, if they saw fit, and if they thought that the emergency called for measures so radical, starve any great industrial concern by refusing for the time to do business with it. It is always possible, however inconvenient or unlikely, for mankind in a crisis to go back for a time to the mode of life in which needs were simple and could be satisfied near at hand. A month of starvation would bring any big business to terms.

But no such extreme course will ever be necessary. For already a survey of the last quarter of a century will show how rapidly industry is conforming itself to the law of combination, how excellent is the result in abundance of product, a raising of the general standard of comfort, improvement in the condition of working people and greater steadiness of markets and prices of both raw materials and finished products. These advantages the world will not part with. The undesirable consequences of the new method have already been guarded against to a great extent; and the remainder will either be remedied in like manner or cast off just as the human system rejects the poisons and retains the nourishment generated from food by the bodily processes.

The principle of consolidation in business within proper limitations and safeguards is a permanent addition to the forward-moving forces of the world. We shall no more abandon it, we could no more live our lives now without it, than we could consent to dissolve our governments, forget all our complex social relationships and return to the simple but barren life of isolation bought by hardship and a stunted existence supported by the chase.

CHAPTER VII

THE NORTHWEST

WHILE the development of the American Northwest occupied but the space of a single lifetime, it has affected the past more profoundly and will influence the future more widely than many events of greater historic moment. It has stimulated and financed immigration. It has supplied a large share of the world's food. It has given homes to an army of workers who began with little or no capital. It has revolutionized some industries and created others. It has opened opportunity for the increase of wealth and for human progress. It is worth while to examine in some detail the causes, the proportions and the future relations of a growth which daily familiarity has not yet robbed of its marvels.

However each event may be bound to every other in the general scheme of things, it is certainly true that the development of the Northwest has a wide reaction upon human life and history. A high scientific authority says that "the central portion of North America affords the largest intimately connected field which is suited to the uses of our race." Land is a first and indispensable human requirement. It is the main support and resource of man. The imperial area of the American Northwest, using that term in its broadest meaning, constitutes one of the largest, most compact and most productive resources of the whole human race. We are dealing with a great opportunity and a precious possession.

It is by no accident that the cruel and rapacious gold-hunters, Cortez and Pizarro, are associated with the invasion of this continent on the south, while the first comers to the Northwest were Hennepin, Marquette, and La Salle. The lowest ambition of the latter was to win a new empire for the king. The highest was to Christianize the Indian tribes then inhabitating these wilds. Therefore serenity and elevation of thought mark the earliest annals of our central valley. Behind explorers and missionaries marched settlers of corresponding quality; men of stern mind and sturdy frame, whose virtues have coloured the lives of their descendants. So the Northwest grew and became the most signal instance of the rise of states and the reward of industry. How sudden this rise, how great the reward, one comprehends best after comparing the oak of the present with the acorn of half a century ago.

In 1850 "The Northwest" was a term of vague meaning. It applied to territory beginning west of the Alleghanies, with Ohio, and stretching southward and westward to include the greater portion of the Louisiana Purchase. Sometimes it was held to include portions of the Pacific Coast, then almost as unknown as another continent. The population of the portion

north of the Missouri and west of Indiana showed
the following gains between 1850 and 1900.

STATES	1850	1900
Illinois	851,470	4,821,550
Wisconsin	305,391	2,069,042
Iowa	192,214	2,231,853
Minnesota	6,077	1,751,394
North Dakota		319,146
South Dakota		401,570
Total	1,355,152	11,594,555

In addition to the 11,594,555 population of this
group, Kansas and Nebraska had 2,536,795 people;
and Montana, Idaho, Washington and Oregon
1,336,740 more. Without, therefore, including those
other states of the interior basin generally reckoned
a part of the Northwest, these twelve commonwealths
contained in 1900 more than fifteen million inhabitants.
Their population was practically multiplied by twelve
in the last half of the last century. To-day they have
millions more people than they had ten years ago. This
growth has no parallel. Never before was a wilderness
of such proportions reclaimed, never before did a
population so increase within the same limits of time.

The contrast in other respects is even more startling.
The Federal authorities who, in 1850, gathered all
the national statistics into a single modest volume,
had not only fewer activities to chronicle but they
followed a different standard. Aside from enumerating
population, they were interested mainly in three things;

the spread of education, the growth and extension of religious activity, and the progress of agriculture. Along these lines only can a comparison be made. The number of pupils attending colleges and public schools in the middle of the last century in the territory under consideration was 274,395. In 1902 it was more than three and a half millions in the country extending from Lake Michigan to the Pacific. The tables of occupation, the opening of farm and railroad and factory, present the change even more vividly. In 1850 there was practically no agriculture beyond the western borders of Illinois, Wisconsin, Iowa and Minnesota Territory. These had 6,914,761 acres of improved and 10,864,254 acres of unimproved farm lands; valued, with improvements, at more than $150,000,000. Fifty years later these same divisions, with the Dakotas, contained 108,216,831 acres of improved and 39,876,715 acres of unimproved farm land; valued, with improvements, at $5,037,720,205. Kansas and Nebraska by this time had added 43,473,145 acres of improved and 28,101,604 acres of unimproved farm land, valued at $1,221,312,790. In Washington, Idaho, Montana and Oregon there were 9,944,087 acres of improved and 23,675,895 acres of unimproved farm land, valued at $352,291,497. The census of 1910 will show that even this rate of progress has been surpassed during the past decade in the far Western states.

In these fifty years there were added three times as many farms as had been opened in the whole two hundred and fifty years from the settlement of America. The addition to acreage was 547,640,932 acres, or nearly twice as much as all opened up before 1850. Of this growth the twelve states constituting what is most properly included under "The Northwest" had 235,509,262 acres, or very nearly one-half of the total addition to farm area in the United States, although all other parts of the country had known marvellous growth. They had about one-seventeenth of the entire farm area in 1850 and about one-third in 1900.

Prior to 1850 over three-fourths of the total value of farm land was found east and south of the Ohio River. The value of farm property per acre in that year was $13.51 for the whole country, but in the Western states it was only $1.86. In 1900 the average value per acre for the country had risen to $24.39, and of this increase the rich soils of the West contributed the larger share. To-day it has been still further increased. There is no better measure of this growth, especially for more recent years, than the following table, giving the total combined receipts of grain, including wheat, corn, oats and flour — each barrel of flour being reckoned as four and a half bushels of wheat — at four principal Northwestern markets.

YEAR	DULUTH	MINNEAPOLIS	MILWAUKEE	CHICAGO
1887	23,649,694	48,618,563	31,960,319	163,437,724
1907	84,550,412	134,991,765	58,928,462	307,246,141

Fifty years ago manufacturing in the Northwest was only a name. Lumber and flour were prepared and marketed and a few hands were at work producing textiles of coarse fabric. The entire value of home-made manufactures in Illinois, Wisconsin and Iowa, the only portion of our Northwest from which any manufacturing return whatever was made in the census of 1850, was $1,420,818. The shops and factories of the State of Illinois alone turned out in 1905 manufactured goods valued at almost exactly one thousand times that sum; three and a third times as much for every working day as the entire territory could show for its year's labour half a century ago. Facts like these hammer home a sense of the magnitude of the development of the Northwest and its place in the progress not only of this nation but of the world.

In 1850 the total valuation of real and personal property combined in Illinois was $156,265,006; it is now largely in excess of a billion dollars. In the same year the returned valuation of Iowa was $23,714,638 and of Wisconsin $42,056,595. Minnesota, Kansas and Nebraska made no returns, their property values being scattered and trifling. The real and personal property of these six states and territories, representing the genesis of the Northwest, amounted to no more than $222,036,239.

The latest assessment returns are incomplete and far from dependable, but they show property on the rolls of the six states to the amount of $8,348,868,366; while the grand total of this added to the valuations for the other six commonwealths of the Northwest westward to the Pacific is $10,739,709,268. These tangible assets represent the growth, in a little over half a century, of land and its improvements, and that small fraction of other property value which is included in the tax lists. The exchanges of the clearing-houses in 1908 at Chicago, St. Louis, Kansas City and Minneapolis were nearly one-third of those of the fifteen most important cities of the country, excluding New York.

Immigration and industry have transformed a wilderness in half a century into the home of plenty. The single influence that has contributed most to this astonishing work is, of course, the rise and scientific development of the modern transportation system. In the early fifties of the last century the railroad as a factor in national growth was little considered and less understood. The union by rail of the Great Lakes with the Atlantic took place as late as 1850. Chicago then contained less than 30,000 people, and the whole crude development of the Northwest depended upon its waterways and upon the prairie schooner. The engineers sent out in 1852 to make the original surveys for the Illinois Central across the prairies found their camps frequently invaded by wolves. The principal railroad lines in operation in the country were from New York to Boston, from New York to Buffalo, Philadelphia, Baltimore and Pittsburgh; from Detroit headed toward Chicago, and from Cincinnati to Sandusky.

In the decade between 1850 and 1860 the average charge for carrying one ton of freight one mile was three cents or more. The freight on a bushel of wheat from Chicago to New York, utilizing lake and canal, was 26.62 cents. There can be no contrast more striking than that between the common carriers of fifty years ago and those of to-day.

In 1850 there were a little over nine thousand miles of railroad in the United States. A few tracks had thrust themselves as far west as the Mississippi, but beyond that forest and plain were uninvaded by the iron highway. Twelve years later, in 1862, the whole railroad system of Minnesota, the gateway to the newer portion of the Northwest, was comprised in ten miles of track connecting St. Paul and St. Anthony. The scanty products of the country were shipped out by steamboat and barge; and had that remained unchanged, they would be scanty still. The railroad, aiding incoming population and growing industry, made the Northwest and added its immense resources to the wealth of the nation and the natural capital of the world.

In 1857 Congress made a liberal grant of lands to Minnesota to aid in the construction of railways. The Territory transferred the grant to a corporation; and after its admission, the following year, the state loaned its credit to several companies. They all defaulted, and it was not until 1862 that the ten miles of road already referred to were completed by the St. Paul & Pacific, virtually a reorganization of one of the defunct concerns. This company was afterward divided, and its two sections prosecuted railway construction with varying fortunes until the financial collapse of 1873 prostrated both. The properties were heavily and repeatedly mortgaged, their credit exhausted. Construction stopped; and with it the development which the Northwest had for a time enjoyed. Up to 1871 some 285 miles of track had been completed, reaching the Red River at Breckenridge; and by the same date about five hundred miles of the Northern Pacific had been constructed. Now both enterprises stopped; and the Northwest grew only as settlement crept forward over the prairies a few miles each year in the wake of ox-teams.

In 1878 four associates, George Stephen, now Lord Mountstephen; Donald A. Smith, now Lord Strathcona; Norman W. Kittson and myself obtained control of the St. Paul & Pacific's lines through purchase of its outstanding securities. The volume of these showed the large amount of money that had been invested, wisely or unwisely, in the original enterprises.

Their stock aggregated $6,500,000 and their bonded indebtedness nearly $33,000,000, aside from floating obligations. These were all valid securities, had to be purchased in the market, and as the faith of the associates in the future of the Northwest was not shared generally at that time by men with capital to invest, they were obliged to pledge their possessions and strain their credit to secure the funds necessary not only to complete this purchase but to rush additional construction of new lines that must be built to save the land grant. The capitalization of the lines purchased and built was approximately $44,000,000, and the deal a large one for those days.

In 1879 this property, then including 656 miles of railroad, was reorganized as the St. Paul, Minneapolis & Manitoba Railway Company. Since the common custom in reorganizations is to increase the total volume of indebtedness, it is worthy of mention, and has not been without its bearing upon the prosperous growth of the Northwest, that the capitalization of the new company was but $31,000,000; a scaling down of about 30 per cent.

The problem of the railroad now became the problem of the Northwest. These great fertile spaces were to be opened to settlement as rapidly as capital could be amassed and energy applied to the work of construction. And settlement, thus stimulated, was continually, on its part, pressing against transportation facilities and demanding their enlargement. Connection was made with the Great Lakes by a line to Duluth, branches of the main line were pushed through the fertile lands of Minnesota and Dakota, and in 1893 the transcontinental system was finished to the Pacific Coast.

By that time the St. Paul, Minneapolis & Manitoba had become the Great Northern; and in 1907 all the subsidiary systems which, for convenience or of necessity, had been operated by the latter company were consolidated with it into one system which had grown in 1908 to a total of 6,743 miles operated. The addition of more than six thousand miles of new construction during thirty years is a fair measure of the growth of the Northwest, of whose common carriers this system is but one. One illustration will show what has happened to freight rates. When the railroad property was taken over from the receivers, the rate from St. Vincent to Duluth was 40 cents per hundred; now it is 13.

The financing of such an enterprise is no less vital than its construction and operation. It began, as stated, with an issue of $31,000,000 of stock and bonds to represent property into which the proceeds of the sale of $44,000,000 of securities had previously been put. Extensions and the creation of great terminals called for increased capitalization from time to time. To a large extent betterments were paid for out of current earnings, instead of by new stock or bond issues. Rolling stock was provided in the same way; and the extent of this drain upon resources appears from the increase of 49 locomotives on the system originally to 1,081 in 1908; of passenger cars from 58 to 802; and of freight and work cars from 761 to 43,890.

To provide funds for the more than 6,000 miles of track added to the system by construction and purchase, the total of its capital stock and bonded debt had become, June 30, 1908, exclusive of the bonds of the Burlington system guaranteed jointly by the Great Northern and Northern Pacific, which the Burlington property amply secures and whose fixed charges it pays, $307,918,689. The growth of interest and confidence raised the number of stockholders from

122 in 1892 to 15,000 in 1908, with an average holding of 140 shares, or $14,000 each. Between 1890 and 1908 these stockholders paid in $160,000,000 in actual cash. This, in addition to the bond issues, represented the vast sum that had to be raised on faith in the property and the country, to keep the railroad system abreast of development in the Northwest. In the seventeen years 1891–1907, all the surplus earnings of the system and $1,366,728 additional were put back into the property in additions and betterments.

The total outstanding stock and bonds per mile of main track for the Great Northern system amount to $45,031.77. Its terminal facilities could not be duplicated for any money. The small traffic of settlers and frontier posts has grown to the carriage of 493,000,000 passengers and nearly six billion tons of freight one mile in 1908. Precisely as farm lands have increased from $2.50 an acre to $50 or $75, just as city lots now sell for more per front foot than their former whole value, sometimes more than the value of the entire town site thirty years ago, so the value of railroad property has increased with the growth of the country. One is as natural, as just and as deserved as the other. They arrive in such connection that each is cause and each effect of the other. But on the mere basis of assessed valuations, the total of railway capitalization or valuation is very small when compared with the total value added to private property within the same period. Both are of equal propriety and validity, and are entitled to the same return.

During the same period the Northern Pacific's transcontinental line was completed, the system was built up and reorganized, the Burlington extended into the Northwest, and the Milwaukee & St. Paul, the Northwestern, the Canadian Pacific and other companies contributed new mileage yearly to the facilities of this section.

Nowhere else do comparative statistics show more accurately the rapidity of growth. In 1870 the total railway mileage of the United States was 52,922 and in 1890 it had grown to 166,793. The increase in these twenty years for the country was 215 per cent. But in those same years the mileage in the states beginning with Illinois on the East and extending to the Pacific Coast, including Nebraska on the south, increased 341 per cent. In the seven distinctively Northwestern states, Minnesota, the Dakotas, Montana, Idaho, Washington and Oregon, the increase was 1,181 per cent. In 1907 these seven states had 27,161 miles of railroad as against 16,863 miles in 1890; and within their boundaries construction is proceeding more rapidly than elsewhere.

While this labour of organization, of financing, of construction, of operation and of traffic building went forward, transportation charges fell progressively until now the Northwest has relatively — that is, taking into account the newness of the country and comparative density of population and traffic — the lowest railway rates in the world.

This mutual benefit can continue only while the

products of fields and factories are carried to the consumer on such terms as give its proper profit to each party to the transaction; thus encouraging the further increase of industry by guaranteeing to each its reasonable share of gain. The embodiment in practice of this principle that railroading is a business enterprise and not a speculation; that its chief interest is in the field, the factory and the mine rather than upon the stock exchange; that the intelligent and just system of profit-sharing between carrier and shipper embodied in reasonable rates will best promote the prosperity of both and enlarge the common heritage, is not the least of the contributions made by the Northwest to the development of the nation and the world within the last fifty years.

So much for the past of the Northwest. The duty of its people now is to render secure its development and progress. The causes of its growth are to be found in the transfer of an immense population, supplied by our own natural increase and by immigration, to enormous areas of fertile soil. It was like opening the vaults of a treasury and bidding each man help himself.

But these conditions cannot be permanent. The present era is the crisis of the old order. The primary business of the Northwest hitherto has been the mastery of natural conditions. Its next contribution should be to the economic and social evolution of the race. We must determine upon a national economy quite different from the present when our population shall approach three times what it was in 1900. Striking as the contrast has been found between 1850 and 1900, that between 1900 and 1950 will reveal more serious features.

Practically speaking, our public lands are about all occupied. Our other natural resources have been exploited with a lavish hand. Our iron and coal supplies will show signs of exhaustion before fifty years have passed. The former, at the present rate of increasing production, will be greatly reduced. Our forests are going rapidly; our supply of mineral oil flows to the ends of the earth. The soil of the country is being impoverished by careless treatment. In some of the richest portions of the country its productivity has deteriorated fully 50 per cent. These are facts to which necessity will compel our attention before we have reached the middle of this century. To a realization of our position, and especially to a jealous care of our land resources, both as to quantity and quality, to a mode of cultivation that will at once multiply the yield per acre and restore instead of impairing fertility, we must come without delay. There is no issue, in business or in politics, that compares in importance or in power with this.

The outlook for our future has been summed up with rare accuracy and force by the late Professor Shaler in these words:

"As the population becomes dense there will soon appear the dangers of poverty and misery that are apt to accompany a crowded civilization. The enormous pressure of masses of people seems to crush out the hope and energy and prosperity of a large proportion of them; and the great problem of modern progress, after all, is how to deal with this tendency — how to prevent the forces of advancing social evolution from being destructive as well as creative."

This is the problem of a nation, exactly stated; and it is, in a special sense, the problem of the Northwest. As here the noblest fruits of prosperity have been gathered, so here must be evolved methods to preserve them from decay. Leadership implies responsibility. It is the central area of this continent that gave the material and the stage for the latest phases of human progress. It is there that the problems which have baffled older nations, the processes as yet unaccomplished, must be worked out.

Nowhere else can be found more energy or more courage to join with great issues. The event will come not through mere boasting or through the accretion of wealth and the magnification of industries, but as all the works of science and all the revelations of natural law have been identified with our common life; by infinite patience, infinite study of facts as they are, infinite search for the right adaptation of means to ends, infinite devotion to the glory and perpetuity of our institutions and infinite love for man as he should and yet may be.

CHAPTER VIII

ORIENTAL TRADE

PART I — CONSTRUCTIVE

THE history of our trade with the Orient is a tale of lost opportunity. Yet so much more popular are facts that tickle our pride than those hinting of neglect or mistake that comparatively few people to-day appreciate what this opportunity was, and to what extent and why we have lost it.

The trade with the Orient is the oldest and most prized among men. Its origin and its value go back to the dawn of history. It built up many cities of an older world that are now heaps of ruins. For a time Byzantium enjoyed it, and to some extent by virtue of that fact became the capital of the East. Later on Venice, the city of merchant princes, was built upon the same commercial foundation, and for years that was the gateway through which Eastern traffic entered Europe. When the Portuguese and the Spaniards sent their ships around the Cape of Good Hope, they took possession of this trade and transferred it from the backs of camels to their galleons. From them it passed under the control of the Hanseatic League, to the great free cities and free merchants of Europe.

Early in the last century Great Britain, following a far-seeing policy inaugurated by her ablest statesmen, took possession of this trade and has retained the lion's share of it to the present time. Her conquest of India gave her a foothold; her occupation of it a better understanding of the Orientals, their needs and methods; and because, through her enterprise and the breadth of her interests, she was able to furnish the most abundant and cheapest means of transportation to and from the Orient, she has held her own until recently against all comers. The richness, the stability, the profitableness of this traffic have appealed to all nations. Might not the United States in its turn become first a sharer and afterward, perhaps, the director of this coveted commerce ?

From the time when a northern trans-continental railroad line was completed this became a possibility. Across the Pacific Ocean, nearer by several hundred miles than it had ever been brought before, lay the trade empire that had been in communication with the rest of the world for so long by caravans across forbidding deserts, by long and dangerous voyages around the Cape of Good Hope or, in later days, by the still costly and tedious Suez route. The teas and silks, the rice and matting of China, of Japan and India, are marketed all over the world. They will continue to be bought and sold and transported; and millions of people in those countries will, as they progress, buy ever more and more largely in other markets. This oldest branch of trade seemed also to promise the greatest modern expansion. The short and direct route across the North Pacific from Puget Sound to Japan and China would save both time and cost in transportation.

Conditions were favourable for a new commercial epoch in the relations of the Orient with the outside world. Not only might its people find advantage in dealing more largely with us than with other nations, but a large part of the vast stream of their commerce might be deflected at its origin, so as to turn eastward across the Pacific instead of westward across Asia or through the Indian Ocean. If this should prove feasible, the United States would gain an advantage not easily to be overestimated; would realize a dream that has held the minds of men since the time of Alexander the Great. It was the strategic moment; the opening of that doorway of opportunity for which men and nations wait.

To reverse one of the great currents of traffic, to secure markets among people little accustomed to trade with us, to get the complicated machinery for such a development into place and working order, required study, preparation, the most careful adjustment of means to ends.

A study of the lumber trade revealed the first favourable opening. When the railways reached Puget Sound, they* found there the largest supply of standing

---

* The Great Northern was completed through to the Coast in 1893. From that time the extension of American trade with the Orient was pushed vigorously in all directions.

timber in the world. For this there was at that time but a limited market. It reached the outer world only in the small quantities that sailing vessels carried up and down the coast or to foreign ports. The freight rate to the East, where alone it could be sold extensively, where the demand for it was greatest, was ninety cents per hundred pounds. This was prohibitive. The question was how to make a rate low enough to bring this lumber to the prairie country and the Mississippi valley. It could be done only by securing an ample and steady volume of traffic in both directions, so that neither eastbound nor westbound cars should be hauled empty. Low rates can be made only if cars moving in each direction are loaded.

At the time the westbound business was heavier than the eastbound, and empty cars were coming east, on which lumber might be carried. When the lumber business should be developed into a heavy traffic, then the balance would turn in the other direction. Then westbound business would have to be increased again, else empty cars would be travelling nearly two thousand miles to the Pacific Coast. While the local develop-ment of the coast country was sure to be great, it would not supply sufficient volume of business at that time to equalize traffic. A market for our products in the Orient, if it could be built up, would not only do this but would be of the utmost value to every interest in this country.

What material was there out of which to create such a trade? Japan is small and densely populated and cannot feed its own inhabitants. There we might find customers for our foodstuffs. Russia even at that time, when her power on the Pacific seemed secure and was enlarging, would scarcely be a large buyer. China is a marvellously rich country, both for agriculture and in mineral resources. The Chinese are intelligent, good farmers, imitative, industrious and painstaking as only a people so gifted and so patient can be. They are also good traders. We must look for our market to the men who live in the most densely populated portions, along the sea. India was at once too distant and too poor to furnish a demand worth considering. But the Japanese and Chinese could be made customers for our flour in increasing quantity. A people once accustomed to the wheat loaf are slow to give it up. And the dense population would make consumption large. Both countries bought their cotton goods mostly from Europe. We might divide that trade or capture it. It was clear that, on the first close contact with the modern world, these races, with their cheap labour and their lively industrial skill, would soon begin to manufacture for themselves. They might get their machinery from us; they would come to us for a portion of their raw cotton. Until their manufacturing industry should be well developed, they would depend upon us to a considerable extent for their iron and steel.

The total purchases outside of their own countries made by all the people living on the borders of the Pacific, including Oceania, amount to a billion and three quarters annually. Great Britain handles nearly one-fourth of this entire business. Although nearly all consists of commodities that the United States could furnish, we get about one-twentieth of it. Although our foreign trade is mostly done with the markets of Europe, we sell fewer manufactures there than the republics of South America buy from Europe. On the other side of the account are exports of silk, tea, matting and other Oriental products: not only the large quantities consumed in this country, coming to us by the Suez Canal and paying toll to the foreign importer and the foreign carrier, but the very supply of Europe itself; which we might be in position, with a low freight rate and an established trade, to bring over the Pacific, portage across the continent and deliver at European ports, thus wresting from the other half of the world a portion of the traffic that has been its prize for centuries.

The best route, the traffic machinery to operate it, the market with its demand expanding in both directions — these were the conditions that opened to this country fifteen years ago such a commercial possibility as has rarely presented itself to any nation in history. Costly wars have been waged and provinces desolated for advantages not half so attractive or so real.

So the effort was made to turn this conception into a business fact. For several years before that, the Orient as a market was carefully and thoroughly studied. At different times agents of the railoads investigated on the ground every trade possibility of the further shore of the Pacific. They lived among the people, they learned the market, they obtained manifests of every ship leaving for foreign ports, they inquired into economic conditions, they mixed with merchants, they laid the foundation for an intelligent, practical creation of commerce between the Orient and the United States.

To build up any large trade with India was found impracticable. The land tax kept the people too poor to buy. The Government could not remit the land tax without destroying its own means of support. And the English grip on the market had accustomed the people to buy from their masters. But reports covering international trade conditions in Japan, China and the whole coast district of Eastern Asia confirmed the belief that here was a market of immense value and that it might be made ours.

The first steps had to be taken and the whole burden assumed by the railroads. The birth and the growth of our commerce with the Orient would depend absolutely upon a favourable transportation rate. Having to meet the competition of the world, we must sell more cheaply and deliver more satisfactorily than the rest of the world. For this, such rates must be named as were unknown in transportation experience up to that time. This was done. The plan by which three great railroad systems, reaching directly the markets in this country most interested in both the imports and the exports of the Orient, should work together for the public benefit was maturing.

The lumber business of the Pacific Coast made possible the naming of a rate that should open to us the closed doors of the trans-Pacific East. The details then worked out have not lost their interest as a part of our economic history, although the splendid possibility they revealed has gone.

At the beginning, the key to the situation was the lumber rate. There were 400,000,000,000 feet of standing timber on the Pacific Coast. It could not pay the ninety-cent freight rate to the East at that time, when lumber prices were but a fraction of what they are now. The railroads could not afford to haul empty cars West to carry that lumber East. It costs, roughly, $160 to haul a car 2,000 miles across the continent. But they could afford to carry lumber temporarily at a low rate rather than bring cars back empty. And if in this way the lumber business could be developed, it, in turn, would make possible later a low westbound rate, on which trade with the Orient could be built up.

The lumbermen of the Pacific Northwest said that while the ninety-cent rate shut them out of the Eastern market, they could pay sixty-five cents and do business there. Market conditions at that time seemed, however, to require a rate of not to exceed fifty cents. The railroads offered a forty-cent rate on fir and fifty cents on cedar, and those rates went into effect. In 1900 the State of Washington produced 1,428,205,000 feet of lumber; only six years later its product was 4,305,053,000 feet, with a total value of $62,162,840.

In the year 1906 Washington produced 61.5 per cent. of all the shingles produced in the United States. And the average mill value of Douglas fir, the principal lumber product of the Puget Sound forests, rose from $8.67 per thousand feet in 1899 to $14.20 in 1906.

Before the State of Washington had direct rail connections with the East, one could not give cedar logs away. They used to let them run out into the sea to get rid of them. Because low rates gave value to them, the price has gone up to the present figure. These rates made literally billions of dollars for the North Pacific states. Resources were developed, the people of the interior eastward had a more abundant supply of better lumber at lower prices than ever before, and there was an unprecedented growth of population and prosperity upon the Pacific.

The next and expected result was that the demand for this lumber grew until more cars of it were coming East than there were cars loaded with freight going West. To equalize the traffic movement again, more westbound tonnage was needed. It was found. Three cars of cotton were sent to Japan as an experiment, the railroads agreeing to take all the risks and bear all the expenses. A delegation from Japan passed through this country on its way to conclude a purchase of steel rails in Europe. The railroads guaranteed that the order would be duplicated at the price in this country. It could be done only by making a freight rate that would get the business; but it was done, and another entering wedge for the trade of the Orient was driven home. A low rate on cotton took it from the lower Mississippi valley, Alabama and Texas, and carried it 3,000 miles to Seattle for shipment. In one year the number of bales of cotton piece goods carried to Puget Sound increased from 13,070 to 64,542, and the number of pounds of raw cotton from 13,230,000 to 41,230,000. More and more manufactured articles and other freight took the overland route from the East to the Orient. More and more inroads were made upon the trade of competing countries. More and more staples from all parts of the United States began to move westward. In nails, wire, machinery and other articles of that sort, a good business was built up in Japan and China.

Of course it all had to be done just as all other markets have been created or conquered since commerce began; that is, by making prices and rates that would beat all competitors. The mills of Minneapolis and those of Portland, Seattle and Spokane began to ship flour to Australia and to China and Japan. To make rates low enough for this, and to keep them low, steamships able to carry more cheaply than any steamships had ever done were needed.

In 1896 the Japanese Steamship Company put on regular steamers to connect with the Puget Sound terminals. But if the Oriental trade was to expand as it clearly might and should, this arrangement would not answer. The mechanism of transportation must be as complete on sea as it already was on land. Somebody had to build ships that would carry at bottom figures. Most of the ships then on the Pacific were from 2,500 to 7,000 tons. To keep rates low the *Minnesota* and the *Dakota*, the greatest carriers in the world, were built. These were ships of 28,000 tons, constructed as the advance guard of a fleet that should handle commerce as it developed. American trade with the Orient should be wholly under American control. No accident and no foreign power should be able to interfere with the low rate and the adequate service on which its fate must always depend.

The business increased. The market was opened, the opportunity accepted, our trade with the Orient, no longer a dream, became a splendid fact, as the statistics show. In the ten years between 1893, when the Great Northern reached the coast, and 1903, the exports of the Puget Sound customs district increased from $5,085,958 to $32,410,367, or nearly 540 per cent. In those years our exports to Europe increased 50 per cent., to North America 80 per cent., to South America a little over 30 per cent., and to all Asia over 170 per cent. To Japan alone the increase was from $3,000,000 to $21,000,000, or 600 per cent.; to China, from $4,000,000 to $19,000,000; to Hongkong, from $4,000,000 to $8,000,000; and to the three, from $11,000,000 to $48,000,000, or over 300 per cent. At this rate it seemed that the bulk of the trade of the Orient was ours for the taking.

The advantages of such a market are greater than appear upon the surface. Our people are so dispropor-
tionately interested in the progress of manufacturing

industry that, when new markets are mentioned, they think at once as a rule of places where our manufactures may be sold. But as about three-fourths of our trade with the rest of the world consists of agricultural products and raw materials, additional customers for these are most to be desired. For every new draft upon our surplus of them enhances the price, and thus increases the reward of those engaged in adding to the real wealth of the country.

Now a new market including from five hundred millions of people upward was worth considering. We could not export a large range of commodities to the Orient. A people whose labour is so cheap cannot afford many luxuries. Labour is so expensive in the United States that the Germans and the Belgians undersell our manufactured goods. But because this country can produce cotton, grain, iron ore and coal cheaper than others, there are some things that, with low freight rates, we could lay down in Japan and China for less money than any other country can. If the Chinese should spend only one cent per day per capita, it would amount to $4,000,000 a day, or nearly $1,500,-000,000 a year. We could not spare food enough to sell them that much.

Most direct and perceptible was the benefit from opening such a market to the cultivators of the soil in this country; to the men who raise wheat and cotton and such other agricultural products as the Orient might absorb. Every additional bushel of wheat sold abroad tends to raise the price of the whole crop.

The law of supply and demand is universal. The price of wheat is governed by it, and fluctuates according to the rise or fall of the visible supply, which is the world's surplus. Cut that down and the price goes up.

Every bushel of wheat, every bale of cotton sold in the East is taken out of the market; is no longer here to compete in our shipments to Liverpool and Antwerp and other European ports. The farmers in New York and Ohio, in North Dakota and Washington must all be benefited; because the surplus is reduced by just so much, and the market price of the remainder is affected exactly as if that much less had been produced originally. A good authority computed the enhanced price of American wheat on account of actual shipments made to the Orient at from five to seven cents a bushel in this country. On a yield of 650,000,000 bushels this would be a clear gain of at least $32,500,000 in the national wealth; a gain bestowed where it would do most good — in the pockets of the farmers of the country. And the like is true of cotton and of other commodities furnished by us to the Orient.

Such was the opportunity created by the labours of years; such the value to the people of this country of constructive work in the field of Oriental trade. As we have followed the flow of that tide, we are now to watch its ebb. Destruction followed swiftly upon construction. Before considering the causes of the change, it will be well to examine the following table of commercial movements. The two sides of the wave, its advance and retreat, may be traced there mathematically. The figures are from the official publications of the United States:

EXPORTS FROM THE UNITED STATES TO		IMPORTS INTO THE UNITED STATES FROM	

JAPAN

1890	$5,232,643	1890	$21,103,324
1896	7,689,685	1896	25,537,038
1905	51,719,683	1905	51,821,629
1907	38,770,027	1907	68,910,594
1908	41,432,327	1908	68,107,545

CHINESE EMPIRE

1890	$2,946,209	1890	$16,260,471
1896	6,921,933	1896	22,023,004
1905	53,453,385	1905	27,884,578
1907	25,704,532	1907	33,436,542
1908	22,343,671	1908	26,020,922

ALL ASIA

1890	$19,696,820	1890	$67,506,833
1896	25,630,029	1896	89,592,318
1905	128,504,610	1905	161,982,991
1907	92,703,664	1907	212,475,427
1908	101,784,846	1908	181,167,616

ALL EUROPE

1890	$683,735,795	1890	$449,987,266
1896	673,043,753	1896	418,639,121
1905	1,020,972,641	1905	540,773,092
1907	1,298,452,389	1907	747,291,253
1908	1,283,600,155	1908	608,014,147

CHAPTER IX

ORIENTAL TRADE

PART II — DESTRUCTIVE

AFTER this development was well under way, the future depended almost entirely upon the attitude of the Government and the people. The railroads and the ships, the customers and the freight, were ready. This country had to give to the Japanese and the Chinese wheat flour so cheap that they would use it instead of rice. It had to compete with the combined enterprise of all the other countries of the world, where production is often much cheaper than it is in the United States. Profits had to be cut to the bone.

The thing could be done; but only if those who were doing it were not hampered in dealing with that distant trade, so different in all its conditions from domestic commerce. From the beginning there were obstacles at home to be overcome, and these grew steadily in number and in difficulty. Results may be found in the preceding table. Our exports to Asia in 1890 were less than 3 per cent. of those to Europe. By 1905 they had risen to over 12 per cent. In the next three years they dropped to less than 8 per cent. It is a sharply defined trade movement.

A direct restraint was the limitation by law of the rate-making power as applied to foreign trade. Over commerce on the high seas neither Congress nor the Interstate Commerce Commission has any direct authority. But their indirect control can be made complete and decisive. A through rate is made, say, from Chicago to Yokohama. That through rate is the affair of nobody but the transportation system that gives it and the merchant who gets it. Formerly the rate was made such as would get the business; because this was new trade, which it was desired to secure for the producers of the United States, and often to avoid hauling empty cars. If exceptionally low rates had to be given on a line of business or a heavy consignment, to take it away from the British or German or Belgian competitor, they were given.

It was possible to make them because heavy shipments to the Orient usually meant cars loaded to their capacity and an uninterrupted long haul. These conditions are favourable to a low cost of transportation. Then the railroad companies and the steamship company adjusted the matter between them. Each bore its proportion of the sacrifice. Each helped the other to get the business; and all of them helped the country by creating it and keeping it for the country. Whatever may be true of local traffic or against domestic competitors, this method is indispensable against the outside world if we are to compete for foreign trade. For our trade rivals abroad are unhampered.

But the making of low rates to secure foreign business

was stopped. It was decided that the portion of a through rate which applies to transportation within this country — that is, the portion covering the distance from the point of origin of foreign-bound freight to its port of shipment — is subject to regulation just the same as commerce wholly within the United States. The railroad and the steamship could no longer act as partners. For the rate to the seaboard must be published, so that everybody could know it. It could not be raised, under the old law, without ten days' notice, or lowered without three. Under the Hepburn Act it can neither be raised nor lowered without thirty days' notice, except by special order of the Interstate Commerce Commission for each case. This is equivalent to a prohibition of any change that will help to get business.

A merchant in Hongkong wants a rate on flour or cotton or any other commodity. He goes to an agent and asks for the best he can get. The agent can only reply: "Well, I will cable for one. After the cable answer comes back, it will take probably thirty days for a new rate to go into effect; and at the end of that time, if there is no injunction secured against a change in tariffs, I can give you a rate. Until that time, our rates as now published must stand."

Meanwhile the representatives of European steamship lines are on the ground. They have authority to underbid. Their governments are backing them up in every possible way. There are tramp ships in the harbour, ready to cut rates for a cargo. An

American line cannot get and keep business under such conditions.

If it meets a low rate, because its competitor is free to make a cut and does so, the joint steamship and rail lines that do the work between them must dispose of the reduction somehow. If the steamship bears it all, then it will have to run at a loss and soon go out of business. Freight cannot be carried 8,000 miles at a comparatively low rate without spreading that rate over the whole distance.

But if a portion of it is allotted to the railroad end, then, first, there is great delay before it can become effective; and, second, since this reduced rate is published and under supervision, it cannot be raised for another thirty days; and, third, if it is lower than the rate charged to the same destination on freight consigned to local merchants, the Interstate Commerce Commission will be appealed to, and eventually the railroad will be ordered to give to local shippers the same rate that it has accepted to that point as its share of the transportation charge on export business. The minimum rate invariably becomes the maximum rate. And then the railroad will go out of business.

So the application of domestic regulation to export rates amounts to just this: that one partner or the other must work at a continuing loss. Naturally, Oriental business does not expand.

There are secondary causes contributing materially to impede or impair the growth of our trade with the Orient. The advance in the price of wheat of late years has checked exports. The New York Produce Exchange reports the average price of No. 2 red winter wheat in that market for 1894 as 61.1 cents, and as 96.3 cents in 1907. It was well above a dollar during 1909, and sold as high as $1.50 in New York after all speculative support of the market had ceased. Where it could once be bought for 50 cents a bushel in the interior of the State of Washington, it now brings a dollar. An advance of 50 per cent., 100 per cent., perhaps 150 per cent., in domestic prices cuts sharply into the export trade. It is especially effective in those markets where, as in China and Japan, earning power and purchasing power are limited by a low wage scale and a correspondingly forced low cost of subsistence, to which the price of the necessaries of life must conform. Such a change as has occurred in prices makes wheat flour a luxury in many parts of the Orient.

The American ship-owner is discouraged because he cannot earn a reasonable profit. The American merchant marine alone among the commercial nations of the earth is unsubsidized, yet competes with foreign vessels government-paid under one disguise or another. So far, for some reason, it has been found impossible to give proper Federal encouragement to cargo-carriers — which the people approve and would like to see done — without opening the treasury wide to the demands of concerns operating swift passenger steamers and contributing little or nothing to the growth of foreign trade. This the people properly refuse to sanction. So the actual carriers of our products to the Orient and elsewhere fare like Mother Hubbard's dog.

Then the American who has put his money into vessels to be sailed under the flag of his country and wishes to help his enterprise by earning the small compensation provided for carrying the United States mails can qualify for this only by having his ships built by the high-priced labour and out of the high-priced materials of this country; officered by American citizens; and on each departure from the home port for the first two years he must prove that one-fourth of his crew are American citizens, for the next three years it must be one-third, and thereafter at least one-half. His competitors may man their vessels with cheap Mongolian labour. He must make lower rates than they and pay higher wages.

The sharpness of such competition is felt especially in the Asiatic trade. As it affects transportation, so it reacts upon the American merchant and the American producer. Not without comprehending the situation has a recent critic of our policies said: "We may build the inter-ocean passage, but unless we turn our eyes to the West and reach out for what waits the trade seeker there, it will only aid in keeping the supremacy of the Pacific in the hands of the foreigners, and we will maintain it for the benefit of other nations."

These impediments to American enterprise are reinforced by circumstances unfortunately such as to anger and alienate the very people with whom we must enlarge our trade if we do business with the

Orient at all. The Chinese and Japanese are proud, ancient and honourable races. They have played great parts in history. In many respects they are our equals. Chinese residents in the United States have suffered personal indignities, and sometimes loss of life, until the matter became a national scandal.

Without regard to the policy of restricting immigration, it may be said that the enforcement of existing laws on the subject and the suggestion of others have been attended by incidents highly offensive to the two nations commanding practically the entire Oriental trade in which this country can hope to have a considerable share. Resentment has extended in one instance to a practical national boycott for a time upon American goods. Everywhere it has produced antagonism to our people and unwillingness to enlarge any sort of relation with them; a condition so unfavourable to the growth of commerce that it can be overcome only after the lapse of time without repetition of the offence.

All of these causes combined to produce the results shown in the table of trade statistics printed at the close of the preceding chapter and exhibiting trade decline. An even stronger impression of the same fact is gained from a study of the reports of foreign commerce by customs districts, contained in the tables of the Federal Bureau of Statistics. Our trade with the Orient was formerly done largely through the ports of Seattle, Tacoma, Portland and San Francisco. These cover the two trade routes across the Pacific from our Western coast. The first two are included in the customs district of Puget Sound. In 1890 the Oriental trade through that district was a negligible quantity. Our exports from it that year were but $3,326,145. In 1908, with transcontinental service perfected and rail and ocean facilities increased, they had risen to $44,032,767, an increase of 1,223 per cent. The big jump was from $5,805,193 in 1895 to $33,788,821 in 1902, before the Russo-Japanese War and hence free from its stimulating influence.

This marks a period in which Puget Sound itself changed from a wilderness to a great commercial centre. Coming down later, the total exports from that district in 1908 are found to be less than they were in 1906, and substantially the same as in 1905. There has been no growth in these three years. Since our carriers have been handicapped, much of the trade with the Orient has gone to the steamships of other countries, using the Suez route.

The moral of these figures is reinforced by the record in the same time of the import business, measuring our purchases from the Orient. The imports into the Puget Sound customs district in 1890 were only $305,289, while in 1908 they had grown to $22,208,814, an increase of 7,174 per cent. The increase in imports in these eighteen years is nearly six times as great as the increase in exports. At San Francisco, where there has been no such sudden local development and no advantage of a short ocean route, the figures are in another way even more significant. Our total exports from that port in 1890 were nearly $37,000,000, and in 1908 only

$28,000,000; a falling off of about 25 per cent. Our total imports through San Francisco were just half a million dollars less, in a total of over $48,000,000, in 1908 than they were in 1890. After eighteen years we were only marking time.

This check or setback occurred at a time when enlargement would have been greatest had trade been permitted to flow freely. These are the years when the Orient has called most liberally upon the outside world. The awakening so long foretold is here. Japan, since her successful war with Russia, has taken her place among the great nations of the world. She has organized her industry with the same scientific attention to details that she gave to her military operations. She has her own shipyards, in which her ocean carriers are built. She has her own factories, in which almost every manufactured commodity obtained heretofore from Europe or the United States is made by her own artisans, working for wages that would not be accepted here. She is preparing and hoping to dominate the Oriental markets and to invade those of the rest of the world.

Following her example, the Chinese empire has rubbed her sleepy eyes, and a similar transformation is going on there. The great productive fields of Manchuria are like our own in many respects. A German expert says that the iron ore deposits of the Tayeh district, sixty miles from Hankow, average from 58 to 68 per cent. and contain more than 100,000,000 tons of available ore. Twenty miles away there is good coking coal. He thinks that the total ore supply of China is not much less than that of the United States. The coal supply of North China is estimated at 605,000,000,000 tons.

All these resources are in the possession of a people who believe that they should be enjoyed according to the law of conservation rather than under the rule of waste. All are to be developed under initiative not only caught from Japan but learned in these years of humiliation and disaster from the nations that have scorned China and done with her as they pleased.

The Chinese are one of the strongest races in the world; intelligent, industrious, frugal and brave. They have several thousand years of history behind them. Both China and Japan have inventive as well as imitative ability. Gunpowder and the mariner's compass were ancient in China when the white race thought it had discovered them. Such men, endowed with such resources as are still untouched in the Orient, working under a wage scale with which the Western world cannot possibly compete, not only do not promise to furnish us with a profitable future market for manufactures, but they will eventually become competitors such as we have never had to meet.

The markets of Europe, our own markets, may, not long hence, be full of goods made in the Orient, for sale at prices so low that no tariff endurable by our own people would keep them out. Then we will begin to study the Oriental trade problem from the other end; perhaps with a humbler and more disciplined mind.

For the present we can sell some flour in China and Japan, until the Manchurian uplands shall be turned into wheat fields. Then China can grow wheat at a cost of seventy cents a bushel in silver, which is about equal to thirty cents in gold in this country. They can do as well in other industries, as soon as their resources are developed; and upon this every effort is being concentrated.

We sell them considerable raw cotton, which is taken and mixed with the Indian fibre to make a smoother and better fabric than they get from outside. At the present rate of growth in cotton manufacturing in the Orient, and with wages in China at from ten to twenty cents a day, the Far East will presently clothe itself and begin to think of entering the high-priced markets of the West in its turn. We have only wheat, flour, lumber, raw cotton, some cotton goods and certain lines of iron manufactures and machinery to sell across the Pacific.

The trade in these, owing to the facts set forth in this article, has not been extended or made permanent. It was experimental. It is still hand-to-mouth and of uncertain future. There was much activity during and after the war with Russia, but it has slackened. Our export of flour to all the countries of Asia in 1908 was less than in 1904, and very little greater than in 1903. It grew 27 per cent. in seven years. The eyes of the Orient are fixed not on the United States but on the whole world. They are the eyes of men who have suffered, have learned, have become conscious of their own powers and propose to make the future recompense them for the past.

Of one other factor in the situation, perhaps as dangerous as any, our country remains strangely unconscious. Probably only the few persons actually engaged in attempts to compete with Oriental industry understand the effect of the difference in the exchanges between two countries having different monetary standards in value or in use or in both. It makes the Orient a sharp competitor.

As soon as capital is supplied to develop her native resources, she will furnish her own raw materials for manufacture, buying them in her own markets on the silver basis and selling them abroad on the gold basis. This will enable her, as long as her own people are content to accept these low silver prices for material and labour, to cut our prices in two. Bar silver sells at about fifty-two cents per ounce in New York. On this basis the silver in a dollar is worth about forty-five cents. The Chinese manufacturer, who can pay his workmen their low wage with silver worth its face, and sell his product for gold that is convertible into silver at twice its face, has an advantage which we cannot ignore or escape. The practical situation is described in a letter published recently in a New York newspaper by Mr. Moreton Frewen, an Englishman who has made the subject his study for many years. He says:

"The fact is, and all your consuls and ours in the Far East know it, that collapse following collapse in Eastern exchange during thirty years has had this inevitable and foreseen result; that, stimulated by lower and lower exchanges, Asia exports to us more and more, and draws her balance in that 'commodity,' silver, which is also her only money metal, and with that metal builds her new mills and factories to compete furiously with ours in our own markets. With a vengeance indeed, then, these lowered exchanges have 'carried Troy into Italy.' Hence we have the problem of the unemployed here (Great Britain), which is so pitiful this winter. Under the stimulus of cheap silver the Orient has awakened to a vigorous industrial life. Given a quarter of a century more of exchanges as low as to-day, our steel, cotton and leather industries, and yours, together with countless small manufactures where the labour cost of the article produced bears a high proportion to its value, will pass bodily over the Pacific from Pittsburgh and Lynn and Lowell to Asia. It is easy to see that the day is at hand when you will be building your railroads west of the Missouri with steel rails rolled in Shansi; that province, nay, all China, is the future seat of an industrial competition against which no permissible tariff will be effectual."

Possibly there is exaggeration in this; but it outlines with substantial fidelity to fact a future situation which scarcely any one in the United States has comprehended or is prepared to face. Trade with the Orient is changing from an opportunity to another of those problems with which we are already well supplied.

Twenty years ago Japan felt for us something of the fine loyalty, the reverence that admires without analyzing, which the bright boy feels toward an elder brother. At an even later date China regarded us as the least uncivilized of the nations that looted her ancient capital and despoiled her immemorial temples for the decoration of modern drawing rooms. In both we might have laid the foundations of a future commercial connection so deep and sure that they could not be disturbed. To-day the favouring moment has passed. To-day the instruments by which that trade must be done are either broken or impaired, while much of the trade itself has gone elsewhere, and more is being destroyed by the rise of native industries to which both offended race feeling and the economic incentive give impetus.

To-day the United States is in the Orient where it is in all the other markets of the earth: face to face with a world-wide competition, with an interest growing but slowly or actually declining, with a high cost of production and with the prospect that its customers are only waiting the time, near at hand, when they can become its competitors. The situation is more momentous for this than for any other country, because control of the Pacific touches our future and unites our fortunes with those of the other nations that live upon its shores.

The outlook is not hopeless, but it is not encouraging. The country needs to rid itself of the illusion that its Oriental trade is to be one of the big elements in its future prosperity — a conception still lingering grotesquely in many minds, along with the idea that we are powerful competitors of other nations in the world's markets for manufactured goods — and settle down to saving such of it as can be saved. There are still possibilities if all the transportation forces, all the people, the Federal Government and the laws should unite to protect, to encourage this traffic, and to liberate it from the bondage against which it has almost ceased to struggle.

The constructive and the destructive epochs in the life of this portion of our foreign commerce are as interesting and as instructive as many volumes of political history or political economy. If there should come a keener vision to our people and their leaders, out of mistake and failure there might yet, perhaps, be wrought something of moment to the future of our nation and its destiny on land and sea.

CHAPTER X

IRRIGATION AND DRAINAGE

THE water on the earth's surface, beneath it and suspended in the atmosphere above it is a very important natural resource. While less than 3 per cent. of our food supply is drawn directly from river, lake and ocean, the whole of it depends upon water in one form or another. Without that, no soil can bring forth any form of life. It is the universal and indispensable fertilizer. But, like everything else in the physical world, it follows laws of its own. Man must adapt the distribution of water, by which the earth's productiveness is regulated, to suit his needs. Where there is too much for profitable cultivation, he must draw off the surplus; where there is too little, he must bring in enough for the support of plant and animal life. Upon such control of water supply depend the habitability of much of the earth's surface and its contribution to the total stock of wealth. Irrigation and drainage, therefore, stand in a fundamental relation to national development. The people of the United States are interested in both in proportion to the extent of its area which can be made useful to man only by the drainage ditch or the irrigating canal.

It is singular that we should have begun systematically so late and only after so much persuasion the practice of two of the oldest agricultural arts. The origin of each is lost in antiquity. Scarcely a mound is opened in Syria, disclosing the site of some prehistoric city, without exposing remains of conduits and other irrigating appliances. In the arid parts of the Western hemisphere similar ruins show that irrigation was an applied science on this continent ages before the white race occupied it. A large portion of the most productive land in England was, within historic time, bog, fen and morass. To relieve the land of an excess, to supply a deficiency of water have been first needs of each people in its turn, according to the topography, soil and climate of the country it inhabited.

Through several generations the land supply of the United States was so ample that every man might choose for himself from tracts where nature had done for him the work of adjusting water supply to the needs of plant life. It is only as the area of public land contracts, as population presses, as recourse is had to less productive soils, that we begin to resort to those other tracts, generally containing some of the richest and choicest lands, which are either saturated or water-starved beyond the point of profitable cultivation.

Of course something has been done from our earliest years. There have been pastures reclaimed from river overflow, and patches of garden along the watercourses of our arid area. The English immigrant from the fen country knew enough to dig ditches and lay tile here. The Hollander sought a soil like that from which his native land was made. The Mormons founded a communal life dependent upon irrigation. Yet it is less than twenty years since advocacy of either irrigation or drainage in this country as a general policy found understanding or support; and less than ten since the campaign of education in the interest of either produced an appreciable effect upon the public mind.

More than twenty years ago the St. Paul, Minneapolis & Manitoba Railroad Company, of which the Great Northern is the successor, took up and urged the work of drainage in the Northwest, and bore a large part of the expense as well. In 1886 a drainage convention was called to meet at Crookston, Minnesota, in the interest of the Red River Valley lands. The railroad proposed to pay half the cost of a survey of the valley if the counties interested would pay the rest, so that there might be definite information to go upon. The plan was agreed to; and when the convention met in December of that year, the engineer employed by the railroad company made his report, and the counties affected asked the Legislature for permission to issue bonds for drainage purposes. The 250,000 acres of land originally granted by Congress for this purpose had been diverted to other uses. At first the Legislature refused; but seven years later the state made an appropriation, and the railroad gave $25,000 to aid the work. One of the conditions of this subscription was that the chief engineer of the railroad company should be a member of the Drainage Commission until the work should be fairly started. By this means the cost of the work was held down to from 10 to 12 cents per cubic yard, which is lower than the work solely under government charge is usually done. This was the beginning of state drainage in Minnesota. The progress that has been made appears from the following facts, summarized from the report, for the years 1907-1909, of Mr. Ralph, engineer of the State Drainage Commission. The original area of swamp, wet and overflowed land in Minnesota was over 10,000,000 acres, or one-fifth of the total land area of the state:

"Up to 1893 no public drainage work had been done in the state and very little drainage work had been done by private parties. From the year 1893 to 1900 some ditches were constructed in different parts of the state, principally in the Red River Valley. Since the year 1900 drainage work has been carried on throughout the state on a much greater scale; each succeeding year brought greater activity in this line, the years 1907 and 1908 being the banner years in drainage in the history of the state."

The benefits of the early educational work are now being realized, just as they are in irrigation. Under the Red River Valley Drainage Commission, $162,412 were expended between 1893 and 1899. Between 1901 and 1907 nearly 152 miles of ditches were constructed, at a cost of $127,749. In 1907 and 1908 work was carried on upon new state ditches aggregating 189 miles, the total cost of which is $295,457. Besides this, there are 114 miles of coöperative ditches, and the whole enterprise is now conducted according to a comprehensive state law; with assessments for benefits, and payments so distributed as to impose the lightest burden on the farmer.

The history of drainage in other states, in so far as there is any to have a history, is generally less promising. Under the Swamp Land Act of 1850 the Federal Government ceded to the several states 64,000,000 acres of such lands. It was supposed that they would be improved, sold and the proceeds used for other internal improvements. The bulk of this immensely valuable possession has been dissipated. The states have parted with the land grants, often for little or no consideration, while the main body of the swamps and overflowed lands remain just as they were sixty years ago.

The origin of irrigation as a national policy, though it is now a commonplace, is the same. Up to a little more than twenty years ago the conception of a Federal irrigation system did not exist. Individuals had done a good deal here and there, small corporations had done something, and there was general interest in the subject throughout the semi-arid states; but there was no plan and no effort commensurate with the needs of the West. Nobody at Washington would listen to a national irrigation measure. Only a campaign of education could bring results, and again the railroads led the way and furnished the means required.

At first three, and a little later five of the great rail-road systems of the West contributed $5,000 a year each as a fund to make investigations and publish facts. Through lectures, farmers' institutes, the publication of articles explaining the need and the opportunity, by every legitimate method of creating and strengthening public opinion, the work was carried on until public sentiment grew strong and politicians began to take notice. After five years of hard work among the people, Congress took up the subject and passed the Reclamation Act of 1902, which is the foundation of all the largest undertakings made or likely to be made hereafter. No one would any more dare to suggest its abandonment now than he would the abolition of the post-office. But it is directly the creation of the transportation interests of the West.

Under this law the Government engineers make the necessary surveys and prepare plans for dams, canals, flumes and ditches. The Government constructs these works, after having secured or assigned to each project the necessary water rights. The proceeds of all sales of public lands in sixteen states and territories, to which the work is confined, with the exception of a project in Texas since added, are set apart as a fund to pay cost of construction. The major portion of the amount obtained from sales within any state — which is construed to mean 51 per cent. — must be expended within that state. The balance may be assigned to any project. The cost of the work is assessed upon the acreage reclaimed under it. This is divided into ten equal instalments. The settler can obtain the land, in tracts not exceeding 160 acres, by paying fifty cents per acre in cash and assuming the deferred payments, which are to be made annually for ten years. Title is not complete until all these have been met. Thereafter the land and the irrigating works belong to the title-holders; and the sums which they have paid in constitute a revolving fund, which must be used in additional reclamation work.

Thus the system, if not interfered with, is self-supporting and self-perpetuating until every acre of land that can be benefited by irrigation shall have been redeemed, occupied and cultivated. It is one of the most beneficent works ever carried out by any government for its people. The cost of the perpetual water right so far has averaged from $20 to $30 per acre. Following the rule that public enterprises are more costly than private, this work costs too much. Where water could be put on land for $10 to $12 per acre, the cost to the Government is much greater. The average amount of water supplied annually is enough to cover the land four feet deep. Only one-half of this amount actually reaches the crops, the remainder unavoidably escaping in the process of being conducted to growing plants and trees. Canada has followed a slightly different method. In southern Alberta is a tract of 3,000,000 acres reserved from settlement. Irrigation works are completed, the land is sold outright to settlers at from $15 to $25 an acre, and then there is a perpetual water rate of fifty cents an acre annually. About 1,000,000 acres were thus opened to settlement in a single year.

Progress under our system has been very rapid, for two reasons. Most of the country dealt with had already been surveyed, and the engineers were ready with their plans and estimates. The money also was ready, the fund having risen to over $23,000,000 by the time field work began. In 1902, when the bill became a law, about $200,000,000 had been invested or sunk in irrigation projects by individuals and corporations, and some 10,000,000 acres in the United States were already fertilized in this way. Probably as much more is now being reclaimed in various Western states by private enterprise.

Under the national law, twenty-six projects have been approved by the Secretary of the Interior, and construction has begun. Over $33,000,000 were expended in the first five years. The service employs 16,000 men and spends about a million and a quarter each month. Its completed canals now extend for nearly 2,000 miles. Some of the work is of stupendous magnitude. To reclaim 90,000 acres of land in South Dakota, the largest earth dam in the world is being built. A solid wall of masonry 310 feet high is rising to impound the waters of the Shoshone River in a reservoir covering ten square miles, by which 100,000 acres will be irrigated. The total area to be redeemed by projects now under way is about 1,600,000 acres. Other projects found feasible by the engineers would extend the reclaimed area to more than three and

three-quarter millions acres, at an estimated cost of
$160,000,000. The receipts and expenditures of the
entire service to December 31, 1911, are estimated in
the reclamation service report at $58,000,000 each.

Most of the land reclaimed is of extraordinary fertility when supplied with sufficient moisture. By
intensive cultivation, with fruits and vegetables, one
acre can be made to support a family. Five acres is
a competence, and ten acres the limit — if devoted to
fruit farming — that one family can take care of
properly. Fruit growing has become a great industry,
the desert has acquired an actual value that ranges
anywhere from $50 to $1,000 or $2,000 an acre, homes
for millions have been provided, and the literature of
the country is full of the promise of irrigation. There
are hundreds of thousands of people to-day in cities and
workshops who have invested in these lands, are getting
them ready for occupancy and look forward to a future
spent in wholesome and congenial labour on the soil.

It is most important in carrying forward government
projects like this, which always cost more than the
same work would as a private enterprise and under
personal supervision, that the character and cost of
the work should be carefully ascertained beforehand,
so that it may not exceed the estimates. Otherwise
the settler is crippled and discouraged. Settlers in
Montana under the Lower Yellowstone project, who
were to pay $30 an acre for ten years according to the
estimates, are now asked, on account of the excess
cost of the work over what was expected, to pay $42.50.

Probably the estimates originally were not wholly unreasonable, but the high prices that were paid for labour and materials greatly increased the actual levy on the soil. This should always be avoided.

If no such record of progress for drainage can be made out, it is because public opinion has not been educated to the same extent. It has been shown that much has been accomplished in Minnesota, because the railroad early saw the need and value of the work. Yet it is only a trifle in comparison with what might and ought to be done. There are still plenty of farmers who complain that their lands are too flat, although there is several times more slope than suffices to carry off the water of the upper Mississippi; who object to the slightest tax that is not spent on their own acres; who, after the ditches are in place, plow their lands across the drainage rather than with it, thus holding the water on the land. And one may see, on the finest lands in the world, bountiful crops turn from green to yellow in a week or two. The expenditure of from two to five dollars an acre would save these crops. It would make land now worth at most some $50 an acre worth from $100 to $150. Corporations have done something in Florida and elsewhere. The government of the state has made a beginning of reclaiming the Everglades. As we shall see presently, the possiblities of reclamation by drainage in this country as a whole are not inferior to those of reclamation by irrigation. The territory so gained is muck, enriched by the deposits of ages. The tracts usually lie in settled communities, within easy reach of roads and markets. But public education has not proceeded as far in one direction as in the other.

The country cannot know even yet what is the limit of additions to national wealth which may be made by the reclamation of lands now unproducing because of either deficiency or excess of water supply. Our ideas about the practical value of drainage are the less definite of the two, because they have been less enlightened by discussion. Mr. Guy Elliott Mitchell, of the United States Geological Survey, has made the completest summary of possibilities in an exhaustive article published in the *Review of Reviews* in 1908. While the ordinary estimate of the area of American swamps is from 70,000,000 to 80,000,000 acres, he thinks that a larger total, probably well upward of 100,000,000 acres, is indicated by the Government's investigations. Florida has between 23,000,000 and 24,000,000 acres of wet land, and there are fully 20,000,000 acres in the Mississippi Valley subject to overflow. Mr. Mitchell says:

" There are seventeen Eastern states every one of which has more than 1,000,000 acres of swamps, and there are twelve additional Eastern states having between 250,000 and 1,000,000 acres each, and there are six more Eastern states with an aggregate area of nearly 7,500,000 acres of swamps."

In the eastern and central parts of the country most farms have a few acres of low ground which no attempt has been made to redeem, because there is acreage enough without them. It seems reasonable to believe that the aggregate of wet land available for cultivation by proper drainage will be far above the largest figure yet named. Professor Shaler says that in Great Britain and Ireland fully one-fifth of the most fertile agricultural lands has been reclaimed by drainage, and that one-twentieth of the now tillable land in Europe was inundated and unfit for agriculture in the eighth century.

This affords us a measure of what may be accomplished in the future on this continent. In Minnesota alone some idea of what may be done has been given, though our knowledge of the statistical facts is still slender. The Federal Government has made surveys of the ceded Chippewa lands, in the northern part of the state, now held in trust. There are 2,500,000 acres of them, and the cost of reclamation with ditches running to each 160 acres is put at $2.75 an acre. Surveys of another tract in northern Minnesota show that 400,000 acres might be reclaimed by drainage for less than $5 per acre, and might afterward be worth from $50 to $100 an acre. There are such possibilities everywhere. The engineering problems are simple and the cost is light. Irrigation should cost from $12 to $60 per acre. Drainage probably averages less than $10, and sometimes is as low as $2 or $3.

For the future of drainage work, unless we wait upon the slow progress of public enlightenment and the reluctance of people to tax themselves now for a

future benefit, reliance must be placed upon some
such measure as has been already proposed to Congress
but not yet adopted. This is in principle a duplication of the reclamation law, and proposes to do for
drainage what was done for irrigation. Moneys
received from the sale of public lands in a number of
Southern and Western states, not included in the
Reclamation Act of 1902, and all containing much
swamp or overflowed lands, would be set aside as a
drainage fund. This would be used to dig ditches,
establish pumping stations and complete drainage
works exactly as is done in irrigation work; the cost
to be repaid in the same way, in ten annual instalments,
to go into a revolving fund for similar employment
elsewhere. There can be no more objection to one
policy than to the other. The public benefit will be
equal. There should be concentrated effort to procure
such legislation. For while there are immense areas
of arid land which can never be irrigated, there is
scarcely an acre of swamp land anywhere that cannot
be drained or diked until fit for cultivation.

If the possibilities of irrigation are more vague they are
no less alluring. The value and importance of the work
are being more and more realized. There are about
100,000,000 acres irrigated in the whole world. Egypt
has 5,000,000 irrigated acres, supporting 7,000,000
people. Some of the greatest engineering feats of
modern times have been performed in the construction
of great dams on the Nile, by which the natural overflow
and subsidence of the river may be aided or imitated

by man. English engineers are now beginning irrigation works under government authority in Mesopotamia, to restore the lost beauty of what was once the garden of the world. Some irrigated lands in Egypt support 900 persons to the square mile, in Italy over 800, in India over 1,200. It has been estimated that there are 60,000,000 acres of irrigable land in the United States. Probably, with experience and improved methods, that amount will be increased. Great spaces of what was once called the Great American Desert have been converted into rich farm lands, and more will be found available than we now imagine. In some places where Government reclamation work has been done, it is reported that the water supply is appropriated for less land than it ought to cover. The Government engineers are unwilling to listen to representations made by outsiders familiar with the facts. Not all the land among the mountains nor all the alkali plains can be redeemed; but the total subject to experiment is so great, the raw material so abundant, that the fulness of its promise will be realized only after many generations.

The need and the value of additions to the tillable area are emphasized by the rapid increase of population and the decrease of the public domain. The latter has almost disappeared. The question of homes for future generations is of paramount importance. At the close of the Civil War the frontier was about the Des Moines Valley, in Iowa. Kansas was still mostly unsettled. Now the country has been developed to the

Pacific Coast. States and cities that are marvels of growth have come into being. Some authorities have declared that by the end of six years there will be no tillable public lands in the United States, outside of the reclamation area. But this view is modified by the great possibilities of new and better methods of farming. What is generally but improperly called the "dry farming" method has rendered highly productive very large areas heretofore regarded as of little or uncertain value to production. In the Judith Basin, in Montana, there have been harvested 57 bushels of wheat per acre, weighing 60 pounds to the bushel. The following table gives the area of public lands passing into private ownership during the past ten years:

YEAR		ACRES
1899	. . . . . .	9,090,623
1900	. . . . . .	13,391,464
1901	. . . . . .	15,453,449
1902	. . . . . .	19,372,385
1903	. . . . . .	22,650,928
1904	. . . . . .	16,258,892
1905	. . . . . .	16,979,075
1906	. . . . . .	19,345,444
1907	. . . . . .	20,866,592
1908	. . . . . .	18,938,886

Over 170,000,000 acres have thus been appropriated in a decade, and the quantity and quality of the remainder fall together. In spite of this wholesale appropriation, or rather because it has been so largely a game of grab and speculation instead of honest home-making, the density of population in the whole country from the Missouri River to the Pacific was, at the last census, scarcely three to the square mile. When population reaches a density of 250 to the square mile, which was that of New Jersey in 1900 and was much exceeded by both Massachusetts and Rhode Island, each 100,000 square miles redeemed by irrigation will make room for 25,000,000 additional people. This is on the reasonable basis of one family to each ten acres, and four persons to each family. Such relief from the pressure of population will be appreciated more as we approach the middle of the century and the total of 200,000,000 people for the United States. By that time the two forms of land reclamation will have become national benefactions; and the work that we are prosecuting along those lines to-day will be the foundation of future prosperity and a safeguard against future dangers.

In addition to its obvious value as a home provider, the reclamation of swamp and desert lands affects powerfully the general character of agriculture, the level of comfort, the life of the community and the health and intellectual activity of the people. In these respects it rises in dignity and value as a national resource higher than by its additions to superficial area and gross wealth. These recovered lands are the country of the small farm. Their value can be brought out only by more or less intensive tillage; by the growing of fruits, vegetables and other market produce. The moral of the small farm, with its greater percentage of profits, is thus kept continually before the people. The farm containing from a quarter of a section (160 acres) up, carelessly culti- vated, requiring incessant work and yielding a meagre return per acre, cannot hold its own against the snug comfort and ample rewards of the little holding.

Where irrigation prevails, there is certainty, abund- ance and variety of products. Water being procur- able at will, unfavourable seasons do not exist and the growth of plant life is at the command of the cultivator. Abundance follows, because reclaimed lands are richer than any others in the elements that promote growth. These have not been ex- hausted by cultivation or leached away by rains and floods. The marvellous yields obtained from irrigated lands at first seemed beyond credence; they are such a familiar story now that illustrations are unnecessary. In Utah the Mormons have created wealth estimated at more than half a billion dollars from a wilderness of alkali and sage brush. As soon as water is put on this formerly worthless land it rises in value to a figure several times what the best non-irrigated land would bring; prices justified by the profits from special crops of early fruits, melons, berries or vege- tables to supply high-priced markets. Towns like North Yakima and Wenatchee and scores of others double their population in a few years and exhibit an increase of wealth matched only by the growth of centres in newly developed mining regions. But while the wealth of mines must finally become extinct, the market town of a district intensively cultivated becomes a larger and more important business centre year after year.

With the more intelligent and remunerative system of farm cultivation come incidental advantages at least as important as the additions to wealth. In a previous chapter the social superiority of the community of small farms has been mentioned. Coöperation and associative enterprise flourish. Schools, churches, telephones, rural mail delivery, comforts of all sorts abound. Life is no longer isolation. Practically every worthy attraction that draws people to the cities is added to the country life. Health is improved. The desert is always wholesome, but the draining of swamps reduces disease. The reclaimed country is one continuous village, with houses set in more than usually spacious grounds, with neighbours everywhere and no incentive for the upbuilding of centres of concentrated population, destructive as well as creative of high civilization. Material comfort, health and social and intellectual activity are attendants of the reclamation system on a large scale. The economic values are no more evident or pronounced than the sociological and the ethical.

The country must come to look upon both drainage and irrigation as parts of a national conservation plan. No movement of our time is more suggestive or encouraging than that which shows a people at last awaking to a sense of national economic responsibility. For

our own sake, in the higher as well as the lower sense, for our future preservation as well as for our moral respectability, we must consider our resources as a whole, and plan the disposition and conservation of them with reference to one another. For they fit into, supplement and depend upon one another as nicely as do the different forces of nature herself. Irrigation, drainage, flood restraint, forestry and waterway improvement are so closely tied together that any intelligent prosecution of one of them draws all the others after it. That we have legislated about them singly and piecemeal is one of our costliest national mistakes. There should be a scientific national plan, prepared by the best available skill after thorough investigation, in which each of these interests should be so cared for as to promote all the others and draw help from them in turn. They are all intimately related to the greatest of all economic purposes, the conservation of the soil and its productive power. Our governing bodies will not become fully worthy of the name until they shall have assigned to each of these agencies its place in the coördinating scheme of national development.

How backward we are still is shown by the fact that no urgency of public opinion and no pressure of common honesty has yet succeeded in taking the preliminary step — a reasonable reform of the land laws. The agencies of justice are employed in discovering and punishing land thieves whose crimes were invited by legislation apparently framed for their especial profit.

The repeal or amendment of many of our land laws and the stringent enforcement of the provisions of the Homestead Act are necessary to honest dealing with the land question. Speculators and land-grabbers prevent this, while occasional Congressmen and Senators are smirched and disgraced by participating in land frauds. We have enlarged the unit of public land for Alaska, in order to tempt dishonesty there. We have made it 160 acres for land reclaimed at great expense, although a large family could scarcely cultivate twenty acres of this land as it should be. Perhaps economy must be substituted for the extravagance now too prevalent in every department of government before we can hope to see it supreme in land reclamation and distribution. But this plain business conception must be restored before the country can hope either to realize upon or retain its most valuable resources.

Meantime irrigation is proceeding under the automatic action of the law providing the necessary funds. Had this work been done by the plan now urged for waterways, by direct appropriations and bond issues, we should have spent at least $500,000,000 of money that did not belong to us upon it. It will be completed by the proceeds of land sales aggregating probably not much more than from $50,000,000 to $75,000,000 altogether. The gain, not in some theoretical way, but in actual added resources, may be measured by a glance at the productive power of the irrigated and irrigable country.

The fourteen states and two territories named in the Reclamation Act produced in 1908 as follows:

CROP	BUSHELS	VALUE	PER CENT. OF TOTAL CROP
Wheat . . .	330,250,000	$291,112,000	50
Corn . . .	553,564,000	290,546,000	21
Barley . . .	89,058,000	42,241,000	53
Oats . . .	208,091,000	92,731,000	26
Potatoes . .	51,782,000	34,503,000	15
Hay (tons) .	16,532,000	120,571,000	23

Yet these states and territories contain a land area of 1,552,737 square miles, out of a total of 2,974,159 in the whole United States, or 52 per cent. of our continental area exclusive of Alaska. They were inhabited in 1900 by only 7,747,192 people, a beggarly 10 per cent, of the entire population. Liberal estimates for our growth since that raise this only to about 12½ per cent. It is reasonable to assume that, through irrigation, the 52 per cent. of our Western area will in the future carry more nearly 52 per cent. of our population than only 12.

The possible additions to natural wealth and capacity for support by drainage are not as easily calculated, because with few exceptions, like the Dismal Swamp and the Everglades, they exist in scattered blocks of land rather than in a connected territory. But enough has been said to show that, as a resource, they will probably be not inferior in total to the irrigable country. Most progress in the increase of wealth in our time has been through improvement in processes, economies in handling, utilization of low values, creation of by-products — by the slow and patient methods that aim at eliminating waste. It will probably be found that the areas which may be either reclaimed or made to produce several times as much as they do to-day, and to bear values several times as great, by a scientific readjustment of their water supply in one direction or the other, have been as much underestimated as the mining engineer of a generation ago undervalued the ores that he rejected because of their low percentage or the admixture of elements which we have since learned to get rid of. We can scarcely guess to-day at the total gains to accrue from regulation of water supply after it shall have furnished its last addition to tillable area and productive power; after it shall have completed its work for the expansion of the country and the betterment of its people.

To the transportation agencies, especially those operating in the West, the subject is of great importance. They were quick to realize this and act upon it. As they were pioneers in the campaign of education for both irrigation and drainage, so they are as vitally interested as ever, and are promoting both by every means in their power. The railroad satisfied merely to move an already existing tonnage will soon be distanced. It can grow only as the communities along its lines multiply and prosper. With every addition to them, every increase in the volume of traffic, come gains for the two parties now understood by honest men to be not rivals but partners; namely, an increased revenue for the carrier and a lowered rate for the shipper. Ordinary sagacity and intelligent self-interest prompt the railroad to support sincerely and continuously projects that involve an increase of population within its territory measured by millions, and of a tonnage movement measured by billions of ton mileage. If its original motive was selfish, it was the kind of selfishness out of which civilization has been developed; since all progress shows that a man can benefit himself truly and permanently only by accomplishment that benefits his fellows also.

It has been made clear how close is the relation between reclamation work and all the other forms of conservation and development of resources. To put water on arid land is to fertilize it as really as to add phosphates or to enrich it by fallowing and rotation of crops. To take away the excess is simply the reverse of the same coin. Both are mighty agents in the work that we have before us; which, if we aim to be better than the brutes, must be to preserve and provide for the generations to come.

It is a new world that is to be called into existence; and in this there is perfect community of interest, because in it we all have, through our children, through hopes that run into the distant future, through our desire for national prosperity and perpetuity, a mighty stake. It is worth our while to work in the present toward the large ends that these labours presuppose, though directly they may profit little those who contribute most; because of a worthy national spirit and because of that satisfaction which comes to all who have helped to open the door to opportunity and to an outlook upon a broader, happier and more bountiful human life.

CHAPTER XI

WATERWAYS

THE life of civilized communities is as dependent upon the carriage of commodities as physical life is upon gravitation. This movement takes place over ordinary roads, over railroads and over rivers, lakes and canals. These constitute the circulatory system of any country. The improvement of the common highway has yet to take its proper place in public thought and care. Railway transportation will be considered in chapters to follow. The value of the waterway and the limits of its usefulness, as well as the means by which the country may utilize it up to that limit, have been the subject of much public discussion. This should be clarified and reduced to statement of plain fact. For all the facts may be ascertained easily if one wishes to know them.

For ages the development of every country was determined by its rivers, coasts and harbours. The improvement of these, to fit the needs of commerce, was a national care. "Internal improvements," in the early history of the United States, meant just this. The coming of the railroad pushed the waterway, for a time, into the background. This was true in the United States to a degree unparalleled anywhere else in the world, because nowhere else has the railway met that need so fully; nowhere else did it begin with the early life of communities and keep pace with or anticipate their growth; nowhere else has railroad expansion been marked by such admirable system and the cost of service been reduced so rapidly and so far. The improvement of rivers and harbours went on, it is true, upon a great scale; but these, after all, were secondary agencies of commerce. Most of the history of the development of the United States is written in the history of its railroad systems.

Recent events have directed attention anew to the importance of extending and improving our waterways. Two main reasons appear. One is the check put upon railroad expansion by legislation that passes the boundary of proper regulation and represses legitimate enterprise. The other is the enormous pressure of traffic upon terminal facilities and trunk lines that cannot be duplicated except at prohibitive cost. The business of the country, under normal conditions, will have need of all its carriers. The public, however, has been led by visionaries and appropriation hunters to suppose that waterway improvement and extension will solve every problem and make everybody rich and happy. Only after a disillusioning experience and much waste of public money will they learn the truth. It is of the highest importance therefore, that the situation should be understood, and that a true and permanent theory of the function of waterways and the steps which the people ought to take to utilize them more fully should be generally known and accepted.

It will clear the ground for this if a few widely prevalent errors are disposed of first. The foremost and most persistent of these is the idea that the railroad and the waterway are antagonistic, and that either can gain business only at the expense of the other. It has actually been proposed in Congress to forbid railroads to reduce their rates when competing with water routes. But there is nowhere any evidence of an unfriendly disposition on the part of railways toward water transportation. There is no rivalry for an exclusive service. Each is fitted for a particular office in transportation. In any well-ordered national system they will supplement each other. For reasons just stated, the railroad has developed more rapidly in this country, from economic causes solely, as is proved by results wherever the two come into actual competition. Some of the facts about the division of transportation work in America between river and rail are interesting.

The trunk lines between Chicago and New York were built and have created their enormous traffic subject from the beginning to the competition of the Erie Canal. It had occupied the field before there was a mile of railroad anywhere in the United States. St. Louis has become one of the important centres of the country's railroad business, while all the time the Mississippi was at her service. On the Ohio is some of the cheapest water carriage in the country.

Its cost in 1905 is reported as .76 of one mill per ton per mile for moving freight by river from Pittsburgh to Louisville, and .67 of one mill from Louisville to New Orleans; but these rates, though frequently quoted, have not been verified. It is also said that rates much lower than these have been made on barge tows during the season. But the quotation of a single rate is meaningless unless we know whether it covers the cost of the return trip, its due share of the whole season's necessary outlay and of all the expenses that must be met by any carrier forming part of the transportation system of the country and assuming to regulate its charges. Here, however, is a cheap and convenient route by which the coal of Pennsylvania and Ohio may be moved to the factories of the lower river. Coal can be shipped profitably by water if anything can. What is the fact?

Of a total of 8,743,047 tons of coal received at St. Louis in 1907, just 155,470 tons were carried by boat. A large part of this came from local mines. Every pound of the 1,155,645 tons shipped out went by rail. And of all the commodities received at and shipped from that city, amounting in 1907 to nearly 48,000,000 tons, only 368,075 tons, or less than .79 of 1 per cent., were brought in or sent out by water.

The chairman of the freight committee of the New Orleans Board of Trade says in his official report:

"It is a well-known fact that the steamboats plying out of this port find a number of prominent railroad

competitive points on their route. It is also, we regret
to say, a positive fact that our boats are accorded but
little business shipping out of this city to said points.
Practically the only outbound freights that are shipped
on the boats are such as cannot be delivered by a
railroad."

Galveston, with no such waterway from the interior
at her doors, exported 14,172,071 bushels of wheat in
1907 as against 5,496,935 for New Orleans. Up to
this time the river has been unable to compete with
the railroad. In the year 1855-1856 the domestic
exports from New Orleans amounted to $80,000,000
and were practically all carried by water. Not in
recent times has the commerce of the lower river
reached $3,000,000, although the total imports and
exports of New Orleans in 1907 were over $200,000,000.
These figures expose the absurdity of the theory that the
railroad need feel either jealousy or fear of the waterway.

The two systems of carriage have developed together
effectively in many European countries; and errors
are constantly made in our current discussion by drawing an analogy that fails in essential particulars. In
such countries conditions differ from those in the
United States in two all-important respects: first,
their railroad freight rates are so much higher than
ours that a cheaper mode of transportation must be
provided or certain kinds of freight could not be
carried at all; second, necessary facilities for water
shipments, such as modern barges, commodious and
convenient wharves and loading and unloading appli-

ances are provided so abundantly that water carriage loses the element of uncertainty and delay which has helped to reduce it to a negligible quantity on most American rivers.

A recent consular report to our State Department concludes with these fervid periods:

"The United States could, perhaps, reach no more practical result nor one of possibly greater advantage to its enormous producing interests than by turning its attention in the direction of the improvement and development of its waterways. The mileage of the inland waterways of Germany, if possessed by the United States in proportion to our area as compared to that of Germany, would be equivalent in linear measurement to 40 parallel waterways east and west from the Atlantic to the Pacific, and 20 parallel waterways north and south from Canada to the Gulf; and that would mean a network of canals for a state like Ohio, say, running east and west and north and south, which would be something like 40 miles apart from boundary to boundary in all four directions. With this in view, the importance of Germany's waterways may be properly appreciated by the American student of this subject."

This half-baked stuff is a type of much that has been written and spoken in this country on waterway improvement. The waterway is to be the saviour of the producer, as against the railroad. Yet most German railroads are state-owned; and waterways are resorted to there as an escape from the intolerable burden of the rates the railroads impose.

There is more freight traffic on the Rhine than on any other stream in Europe. Many of the rivers of that continent carry tons where ours carry pounds. Why? Dr. George G. Tunell, in a recent report to the Chicago Harbour Commission, says:

"The average freight rate per ton per mile on the United Prussian and Hessian State railroads during 1906 was 13.41 mills, while the average rate in the United States was but 7.48 mills. Unlike the railroads of Europe, those of this country compete vigorously with water carriers for even the lowest kinds of traffic. The average rate on coal and coke on the United Prussian and Hessian State Railways in 1906 was 9.79 mills; on the Chesapeake & Ohio Railway it was but 3.27 mills."

And not only are European freight rates from two to four times as great as ours, but even her boasted canals are also more expensive highways. The following table is compiled by Dr. Tunell from official documents:

ROUTE	MILES	RATE PER BUSHEL	RATE PER TON
Buffalo to N. Y. by canal	500	$.0400	$1.33
Buffalo to N. Y. by rail	410	.0427	1.42
Antwerp to Strasburg by the Rhine	501	.0475	1.58
Antwerp to Strasburg by French canals	504	.0693	2.31

One begins to perceive through these figures that the relative fortunes of the two transportation agencies in the United States in the past are not without an economic explanation. The American waterway, under conditions existing here, and relying upon rate competition to maintain itself against the railroad, has not been a success. Its charge has not been enough lower to offset the advantages of speed and certainty in delivery. The Erie canal, once of great practical value as a carrier, has become of late years as a competitor with the railroads comparatively unimportant. In June, 1908, New York City received 1,690,075 bushels of grain by the all-rail route, 1,133,900 bushels by lake and rail and 725,400 bushels by canal. For the six months ending June 30, 1908, the all-rail route carried to New York 32,489,837 bushels of grain and flour, the lake and rail 8,069,466 bushels and the canal but 1,469,100 bushels. Yet the rates between New York and Chicago on which east and west business has been thus divided were recently as follows:

	ALL RAIL	STANDARD LAKE AND RAIL	CANAL AND LAKE
First class	$.75	$.62	$.42
Second class	.65	.54	.36
Third class	.50	.41	.29
Fourth class	.35	.30	.23
Fifth class	.30	.25	.21
Sixth class	.25	.21	.18

It will be worth the reader's while to compare these rates with those just given on German railroads and waterways, reducing both to a mileage basis. He should also appreciate the concise and accurate conclusion of this phase of the subject as stated by Dr. Tunell:

"The all-rail rates are higher than the lake-and-rail and the lake-and-canal only as 40-cent coffee may be higher than 30- or 20-cent coffee, or as rates and fares over a standard rail line may be higher than those over a differential rail line. And it is equally true, historically speaking, that rail rates have been as influential in bringing down water rates as the latter have been in reducing the former."

It has been made clear that the main reason for the comparative neglect to utilize waterways in this country is the more desirable service, in kind or cost or both, rendered by the railroads. A secondary reason is the failure of cities and business associations to provide the accessories without which river transportation is commercially unavailable. There is constant demand in the United States for deeper channels, big dams, every form of improvement that, at the cost of millions paid by taxation, will help to provide water of navigable depth. But the landing places, connections, dock facilities and the boats in service on our streams are just about what they were fifty years ago. For stating the case in a nutshell it would be hard to improve upon the following, printed in a Cincinnati publication, which advocated at the same time the most liberal expenditure on our waterways:

"When I asked a river man, a large shipper, in one of the towns depending wholly on the river, what he thought of the nine-foot stage, he said, 'I wish the Ohio River would dry up; then we would get the railroad in here and our troubles would be over.' This man is a large shipper of baled hay, cattle and produce for the Cincinnati markets, just the sort of freight which ought to go by river.

"The river has 'got on his nerves.' His 'troubles' are an indictment of the river as a highway of commerce, and they sum up pretty well the whole problem from the standpoint of the river town.

"'For shipping hay, hogs, cattle, etc.,' said he, 'the railroad is better than the river. Take the shipment of a drove of hogs: we drive them down to the river from the yards to await the arrival of the boat, the drivers yelling and the hogs squealing; the bank is steep, oftentimes muddy; there are no yards or conveniences because of the rise and fall of the water; the arrival of the boat is uncertain; if it is on time it comes about dusk, and there is the trouble of getting the animals on board. Then there is the night on the boat — dock scenes repeated in Cincinnati — then through the crowded streets to the city stockyards. Compare with the railroad: you order a stock car to your yard, load at your leisure; the car is run direct to the stockyards in the city, and you have no trouble at all. The present boat line is a monopoly and charges what it pleases, so there is but little difference in the freight rate.'"

The proof that the railroad and the waterway are complementary rather than mutually destructive in every well-organized traffic movement is even more decisive when we turn from the waterways that are comparatively little used to one that is a marvellous success as a carrier. The total arrivals and clearances of ships at all ports on the Great Lakes in 1907 were 147,904, aggregating only a little less than 200,000,000 net tons. The volume of commerce grows steadily, when not halted by general business depression. The total freight passed through the "Soo" canals in 1907 was over 58,000,000 tons. Over 61,000,000 tons passed the Detroit River in the nine months ending November, 1909. The ore alone carried by the lake route in 1907 amounted to over 900 pounds for every man, woman and child in the United States. The tonnage passing through the Suez Canal in the same year was but 14,728,434. The tonnage of vessels passing through the Sault Ste. Marie Canal was 17,619,933 in 1897 and 44,087,974 in 1907. Twenty years ago Duluth was a little town with only a promising local trade. To-day it is one of the great shipping ports of the world, with unlimited possibilities of expansion.

For 1905 the total tonnage of New York harbour, foreign and coastwise, was 30,314,062. For 1906 Chicago's tonnage was 15,638,051. That of Liverpool and Birkenhead in 1906 was 16,147,856, and London's in 1905 was 25,867,485. The tonnage of Duluth-Superior in 1907 was 34,786,705, with a valuation of $287,529,705. But while the phenomenal growth of lake business and the reduction in the rate, which was 22.36 cents per bushel by lake and canal from Chicago to New York in 1867, and 6.64 cents in 1907, have taken place practically within the last twenty-five years, the railroads running west and northwest from Buffalo and Chicago have not suffered. On the contrary, traffic in this territory has increased with amazing rapidity; and the capacity of these railroads is taxed to handle business that cannot or will not use other routes.

In the chapters devoted to railroad transportation will be presented statistics showing how far the growth of traffic in the United States has exceeded the growth of facilities for carrying it. The transportation deficit will presently become so great, when business is free to grow unhindered by repressive legislation, that no amount of capital available for new construction or for extensions and improvements could make it good. It will also be shown there that one of the most serious causes of congestion — the inadequacy of terminal facilities in the large centres — cannot be removed by any expenditure. The necessary ground cannot be secured. This problem of terminals at every busy port affects the waterway as well as the railway. Ships must be loaded and unloaded promptly or paid for delay, since fixed expenses continue to accrue. The growth and the cheapness of traffic on the Great Lakes are due in no small degree to the effectiveness of terminal machinery at their head. Duluth and Superior handled more tons in 1907 than any other seaport, and it was all carried into or taken out of the port by a few railways. These cities have less than 300 miles of terminal track, as against 2,000 miles at Buffalo. But at Duluth-Superior a cargo of 12,000 tons of ore can be loaded in an hour and a half. So much better are terminal facilities at the head of the lakes than elsewhere that

they handle in seven and a half months of open navigation more business than any other port in the world
handles in twelve, and do it more satisfactorily.

The traffic of the country needs, whenever normal
conditions prevail, all the assistance that waterways
can give. Their services are immediately important
in two ways: first, to afford a larger number of dis-
tributing points, so that the piling up of freight in
terminals may be relieved; second, to transport the
bulkier and cheaper commodities, that can as well
take a slower and cheaper route, over the main trunk
lines of transportation in the country, thus lightening
the burden that must, with industrial development,
become too heavy for the railroads to bear unaided.
How severe this pressure is may best be seen by looking
quantitatively at the producing power of the Middle
West; rich, busy and so situated that both what it
sells and what it buys must be carried over long dis-
tances. The twelve states of Ohio, Indiana, Illinois,
Michigan, Wisconsin, Minnesota, North Dakota, South
Dakota, Iowa, Kansas, Nebraska and Missouri contain
more than half the farm-property value of the United
States. They have about one-fourth of the total area
of the country and one-third of its population. In
agriculture they are as important as all the rest of the
country combined. In 1908 these twelve states raised
456,521,000 bushels of wheat, or 69 per cent. of the
total yield; 1,644,649,000 bushels of corn, or 61.6 per
cent. of the entire crop; 608,237,000 bushels of oats,
or 75.5 per cent. of the whole; and 144,289,000 bushels

of rye and barley, or 72.6 per cent. of the total crop. Their production of butter, cheese, potatoes, hay, etc., is about one-half that of the whole country. They raise practically all its flax, and the aggregate of their farm products is not far from half that of the United States.

From these fertile lands comes the surplus breadstuff product that constitutes the bulk of the real wealth of the country. They are now only partially occupied and carelessly tilled. The time is coming when their product must be made twice or fourfold what it is to-day. Even omitting their mineral wealth and their manufactured product, the latter being about one-third that of the country, and not considering their domestic commerce, which alone would tax their transportation facilities, the getting of these food supplies out of the central basin and to their ultimate markets is essential to our economic welfare.

Not all the commerce of the interior seeks a Southern seaport. Half of Ohio, much of Michigan, and parts of Wisconsin and the Northwest are more directly tributary to the Great Lakes. But this subtraction will be more than made good by river business originating in states south of the twelve named. The cotton crop is to the South what the grain crop is to the North. In 1908, the states of Arkansas, Louisiana, Mississippi, Tennessee, Missouri, Texas and Oklahoma produced 8,016,914 bales. Oklahoma alone grew 15,625,000 bushels of wheat in 1908. Nearly all this product is exported, and this adds more tonnage to the lower basin than is diverted to the lakes in the upper.

In one respect, however, the traffic load promises to grow lighter. The great reduction in the volume of our exports of agricultural products will soon leave little of this business, to which the waterway is well adapted, for it to carry. In New Orleans and Galveston grain elevators have been standing empty for some years because of this decline in our exports of breadstuffs. As stated in the chapter on "Farm Methods," the average annual export of domestic wheat and flour for the five years 1905–1909 was 113,146,896 bushels; for the five years 1880–1884, twenty-five years earlier, it was 149,572,716 bushels. The falling off is nearly 25 per cent. Within a very few years our increase of population, with continual lowering of soil fertility, must make our entire product insufficient for home consumption and seed. This decrease, which will affect more or less seriously all the items of our present export of articles of food, both vegetable and animal, will tend to lessen somewhat the strain upon both land and water transportation agencies.

Nature indicates that the commerce of the Middle West with the rest of the world should be carried in part by the Mississippi River. In the last forty years we have spent between $200,000,000 and $250,000,000 on it and its more important tributaries without making progress toward that end. Instead, the trend of traffic is away from the river. In 1888 there were 3,323 boats and barges, carrying 597,955 tons of freight, besides lumber and logs, arriving at St. Louis. In 1907 there were 1,330, carrying 289,575 tons. The departures in 1888 numbered 2,076, with 510,115 tons; in 1907 they were 931, with 78,500 tons. On many of the rivers and canals of the country where conditions ought to be most favourable, there is a similar steady decline of water-borne freight. And the movement to revive water traffic does not state clearly either its end or the means by which this may be reached.

That end, as we have seen, is to perform two extremely valuable transportation services: to carry heavy and bulky articles, where no haste in delivery is required, and a low rate must be made to move them; and to share with the railroads the burden of moving a volume of domestic commerce that will soon tax all resources. In the long run, transportation adopts the line of least resistance. The rivers mark the direction. Just as the drainage of the Central West is gathered into the Mississippi and passes by it to the Gulf, so that portion of its commerce which is made up of articles of large bulk and weight will move naturally in this direction when the outlet is made practically available. The congestion of a steadily increasing traffic will be relieved by turning a share of the business over to the towboat and the barge. Here lies the solution of an important part of the transportation problem.

Our waterways will not resume their proper place and office by following the theory that, if we only spend money enough, we can somehow obtain results. We need a systematic and scientific plan. We have spent enormous sums in the past without appreciable results except on our ocean and lake harbours. We must work to a definite end; and our method must be prescribed by the past experience of our own and other countries.

In the first place, waterways that are to play an important part in traffic must be *deep* waterways. That point cannot be emphasized too strongly. A vessel that carries only 1,000 tons cannot compete with a box car. With a steamer carrying 10,000 tons you have it beaten. This is the key to the only growth of water-borne traffic that has taken place in our interior commerce. Twenty years ago the largest carriers on the lakes that could pass through the old "Soo" canal, with its fourteen-foot locks, were of about 3,000 tons. The canal was deepened to twenty-one feet, and now an ordinary load is 10,000 to 12,000 tons. This explains the wonderful growth of lake commerce already referred to. The difference in cost between the operation of a boat of 3,000 and one of 12,000 tons is only so much as will cover the employment of two extra firemen, two more deck hands and the purchase of about ten tons of coal additional per day — in all, some $28. At this slight extra expense the carrying power is quadrupled. Hence the phenomenal expansion of lake commerce within the last twenty years, while this change in its carrying machinery took place. The fact establishes the sound law of all waterway development. It has been well stated by Dr. Ramsdell:

"The larger the ship, the greater its carrying capacity and the cheaper its rates of freight. Vessels drawing twenty-eight to thirty-two feet and carrying 8,000 to

12,000 tons can and do carry freight very much cheaper than those drawing twenty-two to twenty-four feet and carrying 3,000 to 4,000 tons. The ocean rates to-day on the immense steamers plying at our great harbours, which have been deepened to thirty and more feet, are from one-third to one-fourth the rates of twenty-five years ago, when steamers drew only twenty-two or twenty-three feet; and this saving of 300 to 400 per cent. in transportation charges is directly due to the improvement of their harbours."

These results, however, have been obtained not by the mere spending of money, but by spending it in the right way. We must spend it in the right way on our navigable streams and our canals. The starting point for a system of deep waterways in this country is a working plan. The nation has wasted its resources and obtained little return, so far as our rivers are concerned, because its methods have been aimless. The amount and the assignment of appropriations have been and still are determined too much by political influence and local greed, regardless of the merits of the work in question. Thus labour and resources are dissipated in schemes of little value, or actually thrown away. More than thirty years ago Congress adopted a plan for slackwater navigation on the Ohio River, and at the rate the work has proceeded it may be completed in 150 years. We have not a deep river channel in the United States, made such by Federal improvements, except where jetties have scoured out passes to the sea.

Waterways should be created as other great physical enterprises are. The first railroads did not begin in the heart of the country and run vaguely anywhere. They were lines between important centres and terminal points; and extensions, branches and feeders were added as needed. Waterway improvements should be similarly planned. Locate the trunk lines first. Open a way to the sea by the biggest, freest, most available outlet. Push the work as nature directs, from the seacoast up the rivers. All this should be part of a general scheme of coordinated improvement and conservation of resources; including reservoirs on the headwaters of the main stream and as many of its tributaries as may be necessary to prevent floods and maintain a deep channel in the dry season, river canalization or canal construction parallel to its course, and the maintenance of a sufficient and permanent channel for boats of the largest size during the season of navigation.

The lower Mississippi, from New Orleans to St. Louis, has precedence, and a deep water connection with the Great Lakes should come next. It is as important that the order of these improvements be not reversed as it is that you do not set the water running in your bathroom before you have provided an escape pipe with a free outlet. As far up as Vicksburg there is now a channel equal to any demand that commerce might put upon it. The cost of dredging a canal down the Mississippi bottoms, putting in the twenty-five to thirty necessary locks and obtaining rights of way, might possibly amount to $75,000,000. If we can spend hundreds of millions on the Panama Canal, we can afford to construct one from St. Louis to the Gulf, which would be incomparably more valuable to commerce. It has been estimated that this would give a fourteen-foot channel in two or three years, and reduce the cost of maintaining unobstructed navigation in the lower river from $10,000,000 a year to less than $1,500,000. A twenty-foot channel would be worth three times as much. Just as the vessel load increased from 3,000 to 10,000 or 12,000 tons when the "Soo" canal was deepened, so will the carrying capacity of the river channel be multiplied by increasing the depth.

For east-and-west business we have already the Great Lakes; which must be supplemented by a true deep waterway along the line of the Erie canal, instead of the commercially valueless ditch into which the people of New York State are now dumping another $100,000,000, principally for the benefit of politicians and contractors.

Everywhere else, in Europe, even in South America, they are building their canals and dredging their rivers for channels from twenty to thirty feet deep. Canada, always in advance of us in canal construction, has learned the lesson from her disappointment with the Welland system, although that has fourteen feet. She is now planning the Georgian Bay Canal, to be made twenty-one feet deep throughout. Should that be finished, Liverpool would be little more than a hundred miles nearer to New York than to the Canadian shore of Lake Huron. These two main water highways, stretching toward the four points of the compass, should for a time command all the energy and all the resources we have to give to waterway improvement. Subsidiary projects should take later place according to their relative importance, unless there is enough local interest and financial support to push them without calling on the Federal government for aid.

The fatal objection to most of the waterway programmes is that they aim to cover the whole country at once; cater to the greed of every section and every state by projecting a cobweb of nine-foot, six-foot and even four-foot channels, whose construction is supposed to go forward simultaneously, and most of which would be valueless to commerce if they were finished and presented to the public free of cost. Instead of this, the work must be done methodically, in the order of the value of its parts. It will not be thus systematized until it is placed in charge of a central commission, created and invested by Federal statute with the authority to select, plan, contract for and construct waterway improvements. It must be permitted to use annual appropriations according to its judgment, and transform our system into a scientific method, before we can rescue our waterway interests from the vicious circle of log-rolling appropriations.

The question how and to what extent money shall be provided touches the vital nerve centre of any large enterprise and the danger point of this. Some enthusiasts urge that the national credit be pledged in practically unlimited amounts in order that we may try to do everything instantly, before we are actually ready to do anything. It is a reckless, foolish and criminal policy. One bill before Congress recently proposed to appropriate at once $50,000,000 for the work, and authorized the President, whenever the funds in hand fell below $20,000,000, to sell bonds enough to raise them to $50,000,000 again, and to repeat this process indefinitely. Others have proposed lump appropriations ranging from $500,000,000 to $1,000,000,000, the money to be obtained by bond issues to that amount; claiming that the value of the work justifies borrowing and that it will repay expenditures many times over. Against such wild schemes for blood-letting of the public credit every good citizen should protest.

The country has actually been toured semi-officially by a person arguing, in favour of the $500,000,000 bond issue, that it would save the people $238,000,000 a year in freight charges, and therefore practically pay back the cost of the whole work in two years. He does not say why, if this were true, the same people who received their money back in two years should also borrow it on fifty-year bonds. This is but one drop from the ocean of turgid nonsense spoken and written on the cash value of waterway transportation and waterway improvement; some of it the product of deliberate demagogy, but more of it fathered by political hysteria and sheer inability either to perceive facts or to reason from them.

On the alleged saving in freight rates we have not only the ample statistics already cited, but the testimony of an official expert. Mr. Ray S. Reid, Waterways Commissioner of Wisconsin, investigated personally both the waterways and the charges of Europe as well as of this country and reported the results to the legislature of his state. He found the larger use of rivers in Europe made possible not by spending large sums upon them, but by devising craft to use them as they are. Here are his most important conclusions, stated in the words of his official report:

"If modern methods of operation were put in use, on the Mississippi River and its tributaries, such rivers can be made the most economical means of transportation, in their present condition, that can be found within the borders of the United States.

"Every railroad is entitled to a rate that will pay a reasonable profit, and every dollar of profit taken from a railroad by water transportation must necessarily be added to the tonnage actually carried by it, and it follows that every ton of freight that is carried by water transportation at a cost exceeding that of transportation by rail is a loss to the public.

"If there is a canal anywhere on which the pro rata cost per ton per mile, on all tonnage carried over it, would not be greater than the amount it would cost an American railroad to carry it, if 4 per cent. interest on the cost of construction and the cost of operating and maintaining the canal were distributed over its tonnage, I would like to know where it is, that so I could visit it and see how it is done."

Only as people are willing to give up their money for anything is their judgment of its worth and necessity to be trusted. Only then can economy and honesty in expenditure be expected. Much of the extravagance and corruption often accompanying the construction of local public works springs from the carelessness incident to the spending of borrowed money. If the people had spent each year only what they provided by taxation, they would have had as many necessary improvements for a fraction of what these have cost in bonds. And freedom from heavy interest charges would enable them now to spend at an increased rate. The unwise pledging of public credit cuts in both directions. If we once embark on this policy in national affairs, where the connection between the appropriating power and the tax collector is loose and little realized, we shall scarcely stop short of national bankruptcy.

Look at it merely as a business proposition. The interest on $1,000,000,000 at 4 per cent., if such a sum could be obtained by the issue of bonds at that rate or at any rate, is $40,000,000 a year. The largest demand made by the waterway movement as a whole has been an annual appropriation of $50,000,000; and this is probably more than could be spent judiciously. There is thus only the trifling difference of $10,000,000 a year in actual cost to the public between the policy of cash and that of credit; but by the latter the annual contribution must continue until the enormous principal of the debt is paid, while the former buys something, pays for it, enjoys it and has money in pocket for the next year's labour and the next step forward. The country is perfectly able to provide each year all the funds that can be spent wisely on its waterways in that year and bring in value received. This is its only security against the waste of public resources common to all liberal drafts upon the public credit.

The future of the waterway as a factor in transportation can be injured only by some such folly as the proposed issue of bonds for its improvement. The essentials for developing its highest possibilities are few and simple. For the sake of clearness it may be well to repeat them:

First: A permanent commission, authorized to expend appropriations in its discretion upon national waterways in the order of their importance.

Second: A comprehensive plan, including the classification of rivers and canal routes according to relative value, and also including such reservoir and slack-water work as may be required to carry each project to success. This plan in its essentials to be adopted by the commission at the outset and adhered to without interference by Congress or any department.

Third: Insistence upon the development of trunk lines first, and upon a depth that will make these real carriers of commerce, able to aid the railroads in their task by transporting bulky freight economically and with reasonable expedition.

Fourth: A liberal standing appropriation annually for the commission's work until its plans shall have been carried out over the whole country; and a refusal to pledge the nation's credit for a single dollar of this, which is properly *our* work.

To favour and to labour for such a system, even though it should demand local self-sacrifice and the postponement of local desire, is the duty of all of us as good citizens and honest business men. Railroad and waterway, needing each other and both needed by the people, may work together for the good of the people. The transportation problem, which grows and complicates with our growth and with every artificial restriction imposed upon it, may be solved by intelligent anticipation. A deep-waterway movement that shall set for itself this standard will command the support of the people by commending itself to their judgment instead of their greed. It will get rid of local log-rolling and all the brood of those who are "for the old flag and an appropriation." It will complete and make adequate to future needs the whole system of transportation by land and water in the United States. It will place those who succeed in popularizing and establishing it among the most far-sighted statesmen and benefactors of their time.

CHAPTER XII

THE RAILROAD

PART I — CONSTRUCTION AND OPERATION

THE land highway as a common carrier is coeval with the waterway. In the dawn of civilization the trail gave way to the beaten path, and that to the caravan route. As man emerged into history he became a road-maker; the better the road, the more advanced his development. For centuries the interchange of products and the intermingling of individuals from different countries were accomplished, everywhere save on a fringe of seacoast and narrow strips along the rivers, over land ways adapted to beasts of burden and, later, to rude vehicles. Then came the toll pike, the post road, the railroad; this last being still only three-quarters of a century old.

I have said elsewhere that when the History of Transportation shall be written it will be equivalent to a History of Civilization. These chapters contemplate no such ambitious attempt. The existing literature on land transportation would fill a library of respectable size. Moreover, the subject is so inextricably interwoven with our whole common life that it has entered to a considerable extent into the formation of all the chapters in this volume. Those preceding this have shown its intimate and organic connection with Agriculture, Commerce, Consolidation, the Development of the Country, the Conservation and Utilization of its Resources and its relation to the rest of the world. It is proposed here only to set down certain general principles governing transportation over railroads; to rectify some mistakes and to point out some certain results of policies proposed or now on trial.

It is important to realize from the outset how unique has been the service of the railroad in the United States. When the steam engine and the wheeled car travelling on iron rails were first utilized for the carriage of persons and goods, they were used in Europe as substitutes for already existing means of communication of inferior value. They took the place of the pack animal, the stage coach, the goods van, that crowded all the highways between populous centres. It was merely the substitution of a more efficient for an inferior agency, in a society already developed and a country comparatively occupied. In the United States, on the other hand, the railroad was a pathfinder and pioneer. When it appeared here, the only thickly settled territory lay along the Atlantic and Gulf coasts and the rivers flowing to them. The first long line of railroad was built in this country to improve communication between the sea and the interior beyond the Alleghanies. From that day to this the railroad has outrun the settler and beckoned him on; has opened up new territory, brought in population, created new industries and new wealth. It has served not as a mere connecting link between communities, but as a creative energy to bring them into existence. From this characteristic of the railroad system of this country have arisen differences of function affecting almost every relation of the railroad to the people.

Our railroad mileage per square mile of area is about 46 per cent. greater than that of Europe, while Europe's population per mile of railroad is nearly six times ours. The main service of the railroad almost everywhere in Europe has been to increase the business of old centres of population and commerce; in the United States its most valuable work has been to help populate virgin soil and connect new communities with their markets. Similarly there is an immense difference, as will be shown, between cost of construction and capitalization here and abroad; a difference in density of traffic, in classifications, in rates, in most details of practical operation.

The first railroads in the United States had to be built hastily and cheaply. The settler himself did not go without a house until he could have one with frescoes on the walls and a gas plant in the basement; and the railroad provided just enough facilities to take the settler in and carry his products out at the smallest expense. In no other way would it have been possible to open so quickly the enormous interior spaces of this country and fill them with cities, towns and villages. While the railways of the United States may have mistakes to answer for, they have created the most effective, useful and by far the cheapest system of land transportation in the world. This has been accomplished with very little legislative aid, and against an immense volume of opposition and interference growing out of ignorance and misunderstanding. It is not an exaggeration to say that in the past history of this country the railway, next after the Christian religion and the public school, has been the largest single contributing factor to the welfare and happiness of the people.

Of course some of the earlier railroad building was badly done or overdone. Speculative ventures on one side and legislative reprisals on the other brought disaster. Even the railroads of the second period, from 1870 on, were sometimes ill-advised affairs, physically or financially considered. Between 1880 and 1895 there was a heavy crop of receiverships. This paved the way for the new era. It gave the death-blow to feeble or discreditable methods of finance. It welded scattered railroads into continuous lines of communication, definitely organized and financially strong. A large proportion of the railroads of the United States were reorganized and many were rebuilt.

The railroads of the country have been to a considerable extent and are still being further segregated into great systems and groups. This is a physical and geographical necessity; and would have been completed before this but for the vast extent of the country to be occupied and the failure of legislators to perceive its inevitableness and its beneficence. Resources are no longer wasted on the construction of unnecessary lines whose maintenance constitutes a continuing charge upon the people. One management instead of many implies greater convenience for the public, with increased efficiency and decreased cost of operation for the carrier. Up to the limit of practical efficiency, set by the nature of the country and the peculiarities of traffic in its different sections, this combination and segregation will proceed.

The final product must be a number of strong systems, each competent to give to the people of the territory served by it the best service, and all competing against one another for the better development of the areas served by them respectively and the sale of their products in the common market. Each railroad system can prosper only by increasing its traffic. It can do this only by increasing the number of its customers and the volume of their business. This urges it to consult the business interest not only of the towns and manufacturing or commercial concerns along its lines, but also of those who occupy the land. The building up of industries requires the building up of markets for their products. Railroad and producer stand together for the prosperity of the interest they have in common. In this competition between the producer and the railway in one locality, acting together, with the producer and the railway in another locality, acting together, resides the only effective final competition of railroads — that for markets. Public control of rates prevents extortion by the carrier. Thus the outlines of a definite railway evolution begin to appear.

The immense transportation machine of the United States has grown in less than eighty years to a total of more than 230,000 miles, or about 40 per cent. of the mileage of the whole world. It has bound ocean to ocean and prevented the severance of East from West. It has conquered the empire of the Middle West and the Northwest, turned the desert into fertile farms, been co-partner with individual industry in the creation of our stupendous agricultural interest and made possible the extension of our manufactures and the growth of our markets. Its rise has been at every point the index of all our boasted national development.

How about the work cut out for it in the meantime? Our population is increasing at the rate of from 2,000,000 to 2,250,000 a year. The total value of farm products doubled in the thirty years from 1870 to 1900. It doubled again between 1900 and 1907. In ten years the product of petroleum more than doubled, that of pig iron increased 150 per cent. and the total value of manufactured products rose from $9,372,437,283 in 1890 to $13,004,400,143 in 1900. By 1905 it had grown to $14,802,147,087. Every item of material growth means more work for the railway; since almost everything that ministers to human wants, except such products of the farm as are consumed on the farm, must be moved for a longer or a shorter distance. A comparison between the increase of railroad mileage and the actual growth of work done by the railroads for the ten years between 1897 and 1907 will show how far the former had lagged behind. The decade ending with 1907 is chosen because that is the last year when business was expanding free from the check of excesses in legislation hostile to capital, and also the latest for which the complete statistical report of the Interstate Commerce Commission is available. The disparity between the national transportation agency and the work it has to do appears in the following table:

RAILWAYS OF THE UNITED STATES

	1897	1907	Increase	Inc. per ct.
Mileage Operated	188,844	236,949	48,105	25.5
Passenger Mileage	12,256,939,647	27,718,554,030	15,461,614,383	126
Freight Ton Mileage	95,139,022,225	236,601,390,103	141,462,367,878	148
No. Locomotives	35,986	55,388	19,402	54
No. Passenger Cars	33,626	43,973	10,347	31
No. Freight Cars (Not including General Service)	1,221,730	1,991,557	769,827	63
Passenger Miles per Passenger Locomotive	1,223,614	2,163,146	939,532	77
Ton Miles per Freight Locomotive	4,664,135	7,375,585	2,711,450	58
Total Capitalization	$10,635,008,074	$16,082,146,683	$5,447,138,609	51
			Decrease	Decrease per ct.
Revenue per Passenger per Mile	2.022 cents	2.014 cents	.008 cents	.039
Revenue per Ton per Mile	.798 "	.759 "	.039 "	4.88

The severe blow to business administered by hostile agitation followed by legislation against capital, both in the nation and the states, which culminated in 1907, relieved for a time the situation disclosed by these figures. Instead of raising transportation facilities to the level of the burden laid on them, the business of the country was overthrown by a public campaign of malice and misrepresentation. Everybody suffered; and, for a time, perhaps, a lesson was learned. But the country is still growing; under wise policies that growth will increase, and the railroad must meet the ensuing new demands. More miles of track, more equipment, above all more terminals, must be provided. It would be practically impossible to construct another trunk line from Chicago to the seaboard at any cost on which interest could be paid without charging the business more than it could bear. Since terminal areas are physically limited and in many places practically exhausted, it might be an impossibility to build such a line at any price. With all the assistance that waterways can give, the country will nevertheless soon be face to face with an emergency calling for energy and judgment as well as a public confidence so fully restored as to bring out the immense amount of capital required to make even a slight improvement upon the situation.

There are three principal reasons why this emergency has not already become more pressing. First, the existing railroad systems had not been fully utilized. Many anticipated, as has been seen, the development and even in some cases the settlement of the country. Their business capacity remained for years in excess of the needs of the territory they served. Second, the inadequacy of transportation facilities was met

as far as practicable by the increased capacity of railroad equipment. Third, there has been a wonderful
increase of efficiency in operation. The last, by
increasing actual service from the same plant, has been
equivalent to the duplication of all the railroad
trackage in the United States within the last fifteen
or twenty years.

A few figures will illustrate what has happened.
Take 1900 and 1907 for comparison; the latter year
representing the climax of business prosperity. The
Great Northern and the Northern Pacific Railway
systems together serve a large territory that may be
considered fairly representative in growth. They were
all the time adding to facilities more rapidly than systems
in older parts of the country are expected to do. Yet
business gained upon them. The combined operated
mileage of the two systems increased 20.6 per cent.
between 1900 and 1907. The combined passenger
mileage increased 162 per cent.; and the revenue
freight mileage, which represents the commercial
service rendered by the railroad to the public, increased
132 per cent. These significant figures measure the
relative pace of construction and traffic growth. Yet
the number of miles in proportion to the population
served was much higher than for older portions of the
country. As far as increase of equipment could help
to solve the problem thus created, much was done.
The number of freight cars on the Great Northern
system increased 19,291 between 1901 and 1909, or
84 per cent.; and their aggregate tonnage capacity

861,696, or 140 per cent. On the Northern Pacific the increase in number in the same time was 14,794, or 55 per cent.; and in tonnage, 708,293, or 102 per cent.

The increase of equipment for the whole country, as appears from the table already given, was 55 per cent. in the number of locomotives and 63 per cent. in the number of freight cars for the ten years 1897–1907. But this would not take care of a growth of 126 per cent. in passenger and 148 per cent. in freight mileage. Each cog in the big railroad machine, each mile of track, each engine and each car must be made to do more work. Increased efficiency in operation alone could lift the immense weight so suddenly thrown upon the national transportation system. This, also, was forthcoming. The number of miles travelled per annum by each freight locomotive on the average increased 58 per cent. in these ten years, and by passenger locomotives 77 per cent. Engines of much higher power were substituted for the old-fashioned type, so that a bigger load could be hauled. The average car capacity was correspondingly enlarged. On the Great Northern this was about 27 tons in 1901 and 35 tons in 1909; on the Northern Pacific the increase in the same time was from 26 tons to nearly 34. In these years the total tonnage capacity — that is, of all the freight cars on both these systems — increased by 1,569,989, or 120 per cent.

Operating officials laboured incessantly to expedite traffic by speedier methods of loading and unloading,

by more careful segregation of through and local
freight and by such a car distribution as would reduce
the haul of empties to the minimum. As rapidly as
the necessary funds could be obtained, tracks were
straightened and shortened, curves and grades reduced
or eliminated. Heavy rails were substituted for light,
to carry without risk heavier train loads at a higher
speed. On both the mechanical and the operating
sides of railway work, intelligence matched itself
against the growing demands of traffic; bridging the
deficit between volume of business and facilities for
its discharge by ever greater advances in efficiency.

The general measure of increased efficiency is
density of traffic. This is ascertained by dividing the
total number of tons of freight carried one mile by the
number of miles of track operated. It measures the
actual business use of the rails, which is the unit of
efficient work. The density of traffic on all the railways of the United States was 519,079 tons for 1897
and 1,052,119 tons for 1907. This means that the
practical working value of each mile of track was
doubled during these ten years. Of course, density
of traffic is greatly affected by density of population;
by the concentration of business. For example, a
four-track road between Philadelphia and New York
would have very dense traffic. Each mile of track
carries, under such circumstances, almost the maximum
volume that it can accommodate. But the increase of
density has been as marked in the West and Northwest
as anywhere. The two northern transcontinental

systems, for the most part single-track roads, traversing a sparsely settled country and encountering great physical obstacles, have raised their combined density of traffic to 963,782 in 1909, or almost equal to the average for the whole country; while there are certain divisions on each whose traffic density is several times as great as the general average, and greater than that of some lines operating in the more thickly settled parts of the country.

There is, of course, a limit to density of traffic on any line, just as there is a limit to every sort of efficiency. The load that the modern engine places on the rails is all that they will bear. The steel is carrying all that such material can carry without danger. A mile of track can do no more than its maximum. What shall be done when this point has been reached? Some systems have very nearly arrived at it; and, in general, any future increase of load will be carried far less easily than that of the past. Especially is this true of terminal facilities. The public, on its side, has done very little toward providing increased facilities for loading and unloading. In some cases it actually lessens them by unnecessary and time-consuming restrictions. Congestion rules in most of the great traffic centres of the country. The national transportation system as compared with the work assigned to it will grow more and more inadequate. What is to be done?

One material improvement remains possible. The service performed by each freight car is now absurdly low, and legislation tends to make it still lower. The average run of all freight cars, the country over, is less than 25 miles per day. The balance of the time is spent on switching tracks, in yards and waiting the convenience of shippers and consignees. This is a great item of waste in railroad operation. The big loss comes from delay in loading and unloading.

Every hour that one of its cars is held costs a railroad company money. The tying up of its equipment costs the public as well as the company both money and service. If one man has the use of a car for a longer time than he is entitled, somebody else, in the busy season, must be deprived of it when he needs it. But many states have passed laws to intensify the difficulty and evil of the situation. In Connecticut, for instance, no railroad company is permitted to claim or collect any sum from any shipper or consignee for delay in loading or unloading, "for any period of less than four consecutive days, Sundays and legal holidays excluded." Legislation of this sort is equivalent to the destruction of a considerable percentage of the car equipment of the country; and until the country is educated beyond the possibility of it, the railroads can make little progress toward raising the beggarly car service of 25 miles per day that prevents existing facilities, even when ample, from doing the work required of them. No other business is limited in the use of its equipment to two or three hours out of the twenty-four.

In the important traffic centres the area available for terminal uses is limited. The cost of securing additional ground, if it can be had at all, is often prohibitive. Yet the public is deprived of the use of terminals provided, by such regulations as the one cited above. Suppose that there are 5,000 cars to be delivered daily in the state of Connecticut; a reasonable estimate, considering the number of its populous trade centres and the factories grouped in its towns. A four days' accumulation would gather 20,000 cars in the railroad yards. If each car averages 40 feet in length, it would require 151 miles of track merely to hold the standing cars. In many of the states new and more onerous demurrage regulations are continually being brought forward; the net effect of them all being to increase the cost of service and to shrink by just so much the possible daily average of car use and the working value of terminals that the country ought to expand by every means in its power.

In addition to what may be done by increasing efficiency and by calling water routes to its aid, the railroad transportation system of the United States must, of course, enlarge and improve its plant to correspond more nearly to the great volume of additional annual traffic. This can be done only by inducing capital in sufficient amount to engage in the enterprise. Several billion dollars are required to level up the transportation system of the country to the height of present needs. But capital will make the venture only when and where it expects a reasonable return. The conditions prevailing before the business depression of 1907 are now returning in aggravated shape. Terminals will be congested, the number of cars will be short of the demand, commerce and production will be blighted by uncertainty and delay in transportation, and the impossibility of guaranteeing prompt delivery under contracts.

This can be cured only by great and continuous investment in railway construction; by enlarging terminals, double-tracking and four-tracking lines most heavily used, building new feeders from territory recently developed and in all ways keeping open the channels through which courses the life-blood of the nation. It can be done only by a hearty coalition between the public and the stored capital of the world; all available means being none too great for the purpose. It will be done only when there is the same inducement to such investment, the same assurance of fair treatment under the law and the same freedom to earn an honest or even a generous return upon capital that is granted in every other form of enterprise. Here as elsewhere in national development capital must be dealt with, because it is indispensable. Here, as on all the other highways of progress, the greed or hatred or ignorance or envy of the assailant of capital must be sacrificed to justice, reason, common sense and American fair play if national progress is not to be arrested.

From construction and operation — the mechanical side — the road has led directly and logically to the financial side; to questions of investment and dividends and rates and profits; to all the play of vital elements by which, as has been shown from a merely economic survey of the railroad as a machine, its work and the public fortune must be determined. The financial burdens, duties and proper privileges of the railroad, with the reciprocal obligations of capitalist and producer, of shipper and carrier, will form the subject of the next chapter.

CHAPTER XIII

The Railroad

PART II — FINANCING, RATES AND PROFITS

ON THE financial aspects of railroad transportation, over questions of rates, dividends, stock issues and profits, controversy rages. Railroad financing, with all that the term implies, is perhaps, next after the subject of a national currency, the most important in relation to public welfare and national growth, the least understood and the most frequently and passionately discussed of all matters of the day. The time has come when it ought to be possible to draw its outlines with intelligent precision.

First, as to capitalization. In order that it may obtain money with which to construct and equip its line, a railway company receives from the state the right to sell bonds and stock to those who are willing to purchase. It must make its offer sufficiently attractive to bring in capital enough to push its enterprise. This is the difficult initial step. The total capitalization of the railways of the United States is in excess of sixteen billion dollars; making this, next after the land on which we live, by far the most important interest in the country. Its magnitude alone would demand for it proper consideration. Undue favour-itism or undue severity, applied over a field so enor-mous, must necessarily produce the unhappiest results.

The railroads as a whole are not open to the charge of fictitious over-valuation; nor is the public carrying a burden for which it has not received an equivalent. Overwhelming proof of this appears when capitaliza-tion in the United States is compared with capitaliza-tion in other countries.

In computing capitalization, only the stocks and bonds in the hands of the public should be included. On this basis, according to the figures of the Bureau of Rail-way News and Statistics, compiled under the direction of Mr. Slason Thompson, the capitalization of the railroads of the United States is $58,664 per mile. The comparative figures in the following table are from the same authority; the Federal Statistical Bureau makes them a little higher.

COUNTRY	CAPITALIZATION PER MILE	TONS OF FREIGHT CARRIED ONE MILE PER MILE OF ROAD
Great Britain and Ireland .	$272,291	500,000
Germany	107,272	770,000
France	126,350	410,000
Belgium (state-owned) . .	169,140	
United States	58,664	1,052,119

Thus computed, our capital charge is scarcely more than half that of Europe, and not much more than one-fifth that of the United Kingdom.

These figures, striking as they are, do not tell the whole story. For capital account in other countries is burdened with much that it does not carry here. A large part of the capitalization of foreign railways represents money paid for such improvements as are paid for in this country out of current revenue. The betterments mentioned in the last chapter as part of the development of the American railroad cost immense sums. European managements add this to capital account, thus placing the burden upon posterity and steadily increasing the total upon which a return must be earned. The practice of American roads is, wherever possible, to meet these demands out of ordinary receipts; to charge off a fair amount each year for depreciation; to maintain the property at its own cost; and thus to appropriate to the future service of the people large amounts every year which could, without the slightest legal impropriety, be added to the dividends paid to stockholders; amounts which are so disposed of in most other countries of the world. Those who have thus put their money back into the property, instead of increasing its capitalization, are entitled to the same return upon it as to that represented by stocks and bonds.

Of course capitalization, both aggregate and per mile, will increase, just as land values do. With the growth of the country and of business, some betterments have to be made on a scale so great that it would bankrupt any system to pay them out of current revenue. Double tracks must take the place of single. A new passenger terminal may cost from $30,000,000 up. As similar expenditures fall on all the systems, with the development of their territory, credit must be invoked, as justly and necessarily as it was for original construction.

Neither this increase of capitalization nor any other, however, since the public is an interested party, should be left entirely to private determination. Near the close of the chapter on "Consolidation in Industry," the general principle is stated that the public, both as investor and as rate-payer, should be protected against misrepresentation by governmental supervision of the issue of new securities. No more need be said here than to repeat and refer the reader to that safe general rule, applying to railroads in common with all other large corporations that offer stock and bonds for sale and whose prices for commodities or services are influenced to some extent by the total of these that they have outstanding. Stocks should be issued only for legitimate purposes, disposed of at not less than par and paid for in cash or property at actual value.

Second, as to profits and rates. The money received from the sale of bonds and stock having been put into railway construction and equipment, the company has a right to earn sufficient net revenue to meet its interest and dividend obligations. And it is to the public interest that this amount should be derived from a large volume of traffic at a low rate rather than from a small volume of traffic at a high rate. These corollaries of the creation of any railroad property lead at once to the heart of the matter — the question of rates. What rate is a carrier entitled to charge for its services? Who shall fix it? What authority is entitled to pass upon it before it goes into effect? Where nothing has been guaranteed, what rate is the investor entitled to receive as profit upon his capital? About these queries gathers a whole library of more or less academic discussion. It will be impossible to do more, within the narrow scope of these chapters, than to lay down a few broad general principles that must eventually govern rate-making. For this is not a matter that passion or prejudice can determine; but a branch of the science of economics, under the rule of fixed economic law.

The railroad company is interested in obtaining a rate that in addition to the cost of taxes and a proper allowance for maintenance and other necessary charges, will pay interest on its bonds and fair dividends on its stock. The customer is interested in obtaining a rate as low as possible; the maximum that he can pay being one that will enable him to market his products at a living profit. There is thus disclosed at the outset, to one who will stop a moment and think about it, a vital common interest between the two parties. A railroad can increase its profits only, as a rule, by increasing its receipts. Since rates cannot rise above a certain point without becoming prohibitive, their proceeds must be increased by increasing the volume of business. Within limits, the multiplier is fixed; but the multiplicand may vary almost without limits. The volume of business grows

only as acre after acre of the country served is occupied
and made to yield its greatest contribution of wealth;
and as manufacturing and other industries arise in
answer to the new demands so created. To bring
this about, such rates must be made as will permit
every industry proper to the territory in question to
be carried on at a profit. A higher rate defeats itself
by checking industry. A rate too low to return a
living profit would prevent the carrier from giving
adequate service, would ultimately destroy it and
thus injure the people just as surely as one too high.

It thus becomes logically evident that there must
be a system of rates, if it can be ascertained, which
is for the greatest good of both parties; which will
secure to the railroad the greatest volume of business
and the largest net return consistent with equal benefits
to the producer and shipper; encouraging the latter
to continue their industry and others to join them.
The ascertainment of such a rate has been for many
years the study of every railroad manage.nent worthy
of the name. It has been the professed object of
legislation. Its adjustment has been hindered more
by passion and political demagogy on one side than
it has by self-interest or the exercise of arbitrary power
on the other. This ultimate desire of everybody is
the thing known as a "just and reasonable rate."

What, then, is a "just and reasonable rate"? It
has to be arrived at practically and experimentally.
The highest rate that could be charged is one that
would absorb the whole value added to any commodity,

over cost of production, by transporting it. The lowest rate imposed could not be less than the cost of service, plus a reasonable compensation for the use of the property. The reasonable rate will be found where the interests of the two parties are most evenly balanced. And it is already clear that the value which the service confers on the commodities and the labours of the shipper is a more important element in determining reasonableness than is the cost of the service to the carrier.

According to common opinion, one of the first essentials of a reasonable rate is that it shall contain no discrimination between either persons or places. In the abstract this principle is right. Yet the numerous and important exceptions that always have been and always will be made to it show how empirical practical rate-making is; how necessary it is to experiment, to cut and fit and judge by conditions and results, instead of trying to enforce hard and fast rules regardless of consequences.

Thus commodity rates all over the country have been determined less by the cost of service than by the public interest. Take the Northwest as an illustration. The most important thing to its farmers is a low rate on wheat. Take the case of a farmer with one hundred acres of wheat yielding, say, twenty bushels to the acre, 2,000 bushels or 60 tons. A reduction of five cents a hundred, or a dollar a ton, in his transportation charge would amount to him to $60 per annum. If he visits the country store once a week for fifty-two

weeks and takes away from the store each week fifty
pounds of merchandise, in a year he will have taken
2,600 pounds, the entire freight on which would not
have averaged over 40 cents a hundred, or $10.40;
so that, if the railroad carried the merchandise for
nothing, and charged an additional five cents a hundred
on his grain, the farmer would be worse off by nearly
$50 a year. Consequently wheat rates have been made
relatively lower there than in other parts of the country,
and relatively lower than those on merchandise. This
is literally discrimination of both kinds; yet it is not
only unobjectionable, but highly necessary to the
prosperity of the people and the development of the
country.

In the early stages, both mining and manufacturing
interests have to be helped by low rates or frequently
they would collapse. Grain, coal, lumber, brick—these
and like commodities are carried at rates discriminatory
if the cost of service only is taken into account. There
is not a railroad commission in the country that does
not uphold this form of discrimination as just and
reasonable. Similarly, all authorities have confirmed
the principle that the existence of water competition
may justify the imposition of a lower rate for the long
haul than the short, although this form of discrimination was first and most vehemently complained of.
The rate made on lumber from the Pacific Coast,
described in the chapters on "Oriental Trade," was
discriminatory if compared with rates on other commodities and judged by ordinary standards. Its

beneficent effect in increasing traffic, developing the country and opening new markets under existing conditions was its practical justification.

Competition, as formerly understood, may change the basis of the reasonable rate unfavourably. If there are two roads to be operated and maintained where one could do the business, the traffic must bear the burden of supporting both, and the basis of the reasonable rate is necessarily raised. Rate wars and rates below the reasonable level simply run up bills for the people to pay. For all charges of every sort are, in the end, paid by the people. There was a time, perhaps, when railways overcharged the people at non-competitive points, but that time has now passed. The evil is prevented both by business prudence and by the law. Therefore the reasonableness of rates is promoted to-day by having the transportation work of the country performed by the smallest number of carriers that can handle it effectively. The cost to the public of getting this work done is thus reduced to the minimum.

Almost every rate has to justify itself. Rates fixed according to theories or abstract general principles are frequently impracticable and would be destructive of business if they were enforced. A railroad's total expenditure cannot be distributed over millions of items; and no one can say just what it costs to haul most commodities in general use any particular distance. If you are in a timber country, you must favour the timber; if you are in a mineral country, you must favour the mineral; if in an agricultural country you must favour soil products, because they are the foundation of all industry and all business. The railroad has to carry to some market the natural resources of the country that it serves. It must enable the man who lives on the farm or works in the forest or in the mine to carry on his work, or he will cease to work; and then the investment in the railroad becomes worthless. Since a railroad is always trying to increase its traffic, it must make rates such as will encourage the marketing of the largest volume of commodities. This is the fundamental law underlying all rate-making; presenting to the rate-maker a separate problem for each system and not infrequently for each commodity.

Of course, in a rough and general way, the average scale of rates is based upon the aggregate cost of service. This has been seen to depend largely upon the density of traffic. If $100,000 has to be raised and there are 100,000 tons of freight to be carried, it is obvious that there must be a profit of one dollar per ton; but if the total of freight carried can be raised to 200,000 tons, a profit of fifty cents will give the same revenue; while an increase to 500,000 tons would permit the profit per ton to be cut to twenty cents. There is an equally variable factor on the other side. The courts all agree that a reasonable rate must be such as will pay expenses and a fair return on the value of the property. But the latter is not easy to ascertain. In many cases it is greatly in

excess of capitalization, owing to investment not represented and to increase in land and terminal values.
One complication succeeds another when an effort is
made to arrive abstractly at some general formula from
which the "just and reasonable rate" may be derived.
On the whole, the railroad managers of this country
have done well in their effort to discover it practically
by the exercise of the initiative in rate-making still
permitted them. This will appear clearly enough
when railway rates in the United States are compared
with those of other countries.

The two impressive facts about freight rates in the
United States are that they have declined steadily
and rapidly, and that they are now the lowest in the
world. In 1890, by the Government statistics, the
revenue per ton mile was .927 of a cent for the whole
country. In 1907 it had fallen to .759. During the
very time when the prices of all kinds of commodities
were rising from 10 to 60 per cent., and while the
wages of labour were greatly increased, the amount
charged by the railroads of the country for the important service they render suffered this great decline.
It does not look large when expressed in mills, but
apply it to the tonnage of the country and see what it
would amount to. Take by way of illustration the
figures for the Great Northern system alone for the
last eighteen years. The freight revenue collected in
1909 was, in round numbers, thirty-nine million dollars;
while the revenue from the same business, if it had
paid the rate charged in 1881, would have been one

hundred and thirty-nine millions. The saving from rate reduction for 1909 is, therefore, approximately one hundred million dollars. But if the whole period between 1881 and 1909 is taken, and the rates in force in 1881 are applied to it, then the difference between the amount so obtained and the income actually received is found to exceed one billion dollars. This is the saving to shippers by reduced rates on a single system in the last eighteen years.

The amount saved for the people of the whole country in the same time, calculated upon its gross business, seems almost incredible. For the year 1906, according to the Bureau of Railway News and Statistics, the people of Great Britain and Ireland paid approximately 2.34 cents for each ton of goods carried one mile. If that rate were applied to the freight carried by all American railways in 1907, their bill would have been $5,536,472,527. American shippers saved $3,712,820,618, or more than the total value of the foreign commerce of the United States, in a single year by the low cost of transportation in this country as compared with Great Britain. Of all the economic advantages realized by the people in the last fifty years, nothing can compare in importance and in cash value with the progressive reductions in the cost of transportation by the railways.

Very striking is a comparison between the rates charged by the railroads of this and those of other countries for a similar service. The average passenger rate in the United States has been brought down to a

trifle over two cents a mile, and many attempts have
been made to fix it at the latter figure in different states
by law, although the courts have generally found two
cents unreasonable. This is a little higher than the average charge in some European countries, for the reasons
that, where population is dense, a lower rate is possible;
and that the bulk of the travel goes third class, sub-
mitting for cheapness to a discrimination that would
not be tolerated here. But the important element in
transportation is the freight rate. The average charge
in the United States in 1907 is given by the Interstate
Commerce Commission as .759 of a cent. The average
receipts per ton per mile in all the countries of Europe,
together with India, Canada, the Argentine, Japan
and New South Wales, is 1.36 cents. In Great Britain
it is 2.31 cents, in Germany 1.41, in France 1.46 and
in Austria 1.49. Both absolutely and relatively the
low rates on American railways are one of the most
wonderful achievements of American enterprise. The
opinion of unprejudiced experts is that these rates as
a whole are now too low.

A comparison between the wages of railway employees in the United States and in other countries discovers
contrasts as striking as have been shown to exist in
capitalization and in rates. According to the latest
report of the Bureau of Railway News and Statistics,
the average annual wage of each employee of all the
railroads of the German Empire was $352. The
average wage for the same year in Great Britain and
Ireland was $261. In the United States it was $641.

The American railway pays the highest wages in the world, out of the lowest rates in the world, after having set down to capital account the lowest capitalization per mile of all the great countries of the world. No other occupation and no other employer of labour in the country can match this record.

The persons directly employed by the railways of the country number between a million and a half and two millions. The total compensation paid to the railway employees in the United States is over one billion dollars annually. The wages of this form of labour are continually increasing. The payroll is the main expense item of all railroads. In 1908 labour absorbed 43.38 per cent. of the gross earnings of the railways of this country, as against 41.42 per cent. in 1907 and 40.02 in 1906. When business falls off, wages can never be reduced correspondingly; and when business improves, the cost of labour always keeps a little in advance.

These men all live comfortably, which is as it should be. The wage rate enables them to spend liberally for their families. Their consumption is an important factor in creating employment for other industries and raising the general level of prosperity. But continually increased pay and decreased working hours for the employee mean increased cost to the employer. The people must expect to make good the deficit through an increase in rates. A railway can pay out only what it takes in. It takes in nothing except what the public pays to it for service. The logical conclusion, that every concession to employees must in time be reflected in a rise in rates and paid for by the people, is one which they too often shirk.

The other side of the rate question considers what rate of profit should be received by the investor in railway property. For no freight rate will be "just" or "reasonable" that does not bring him a fair return for the use of his capital and his risk. In any other business, the profit earned by capital is not a cause of reproach or public agitation. Manufacturing concerns, trading houses, banks, are allowed to make what they can. Frequently the profit is large enough to repay the entire original investment every few years. In addition to that, the property itself becomes more valuable. Any man could name several corporations that declare annually dividends to an amount which no railroad director would dare to propose, and which no railroad in this country is now or is ever likely to be in a position to pay. Even the banks, which are accountable to state and national regulation, and have been mentioned as models to which the railroads might be required to conform, pay as big dividends on their capital as they can, without being censured or having their interest rates lowered by law.

The risks of railroad investment are greater than those of any form of trade. As Professor McPherson has justly said: "Many issues of stock represent the hazard in an enterprise and depend entirely for any value they may have upon the possibilities of the future. It follows that the only market value possessed by such issues arises from the opinion of would-be purchasers that the development of the traffic and consequent increase in the earnings of the corporation will at some future time result in the payment of dividends." If a railroad is unprofitable, the creditors throw it into a receivership and turn it over to new owners. But if it is profitable, the company that declares a dividend much above the market rate for loans backed by unimpeachable collateral, or that wisely accumulates a surplus as a safeguard against lean years to come, is ordered to reduce its rates. Neither the direct profit from a railroad's operation nor what is called in economics "the unearned increment" passes unchallenged. It has to fight through the courts for the right to its own property, and the right even to a moderate return upon it.

How modest that return is, few of those whose imaginations are stuffed with tales of the vast gains from railway operations have ever realized. Individuals here and there, by superior energy, sagacity or good fortune, sometimes by all combined, amass large fortunes. But how has capital so employed fared as a whole? Here again a comparison between the United States and other countries is enlightening. It has been seen that the capitalization of European railways runs from about twice to nearly five times that of the railways of the United States. Therefore the return on the latter ought to be proportionately higher. Exactly the opposite is the case. The percentage of net earnings available for distribution on the immense capitalization of the railroad systems of England is 3.47; in France, 4.37; in Germany, 6.14. In the United States it averages but 4.12 per cent. The distribution of gross earnings, as shown by the following table, giving the division in 1907, is just as eloquent of the difference in conditions:

COUNTRY	PERCENTAGE OF EARNINGS TO CAPITAL	TO LABOUR
United States	21	41
England	37	27
Germany	35	34
France	46	31

Setting aside the interest on bonds, which is an obligatory charge, the total dividends paid by the railways of the United States in 1907 amounted to a little less than 12 per cent. of the gross earnings. If American railways were as highly capitalized per mile as those of Great Britain, it would have taken $2,500,000,000, or more than their entire gross earnings in 1908, to pay 4 per cent. upon that capital.

It is only right, and it is essential to the continuance of the service which the people expect from the railways, that they be permitted to earn a proper profit. Just what that term may cover is no more mathematically fixed than is the meaning of "a just and reasonable rate." It depends on the original cost of a system; on what it would cost to reproduce it; on what it may have been necessary to put into it from time to time to make it equal to demands upon it; on present value;

on the amount and continuance of the risk to capital involved in such investment; and on the reward which it may be necessary to offer to capital now in order to pursuade it to furnish sufficient amounts for those betterments, additions and extensions that are just as necessary as was the first construction. It seems probable that, in view of the facts, the courts hereafter will place a more liberal construction than either the public or railway managements have been inclined to put in the past upon that uncertain term, "a fair rate of profit."

The average rate of dividends on all the dividend-paying railway stock in the United States in 1907 was 6.23 per cent. That was the year of greatest railway prosperity ever seen in this country. Yet 32.73 per cent. of all railway stocks, substantially one-third of the whole, paid nothing at all. In the meanwhile the amount exacted by the public in return for the privilege of holding property and doing business — the total of railroad taxation — rose from $47,415,433 in 1900 to $80,000,000 in 1907, or over 70 per cent.; from $255 per mile of line to $367. It is not possible to curtail forever the income of any form of enterprise while increasing its burdens. A fair and reasonable profit is just as essential, in the long run, to the public's interest as a fair and reasonable freight rate. Unless this fact is realized practically in public opinion and in legislation, investment in railway enterprises will so diminish that the country must suffer seriously both in present convenience and in future growth.

By referring again to the table showing how far the
extension of railway facilities in the last ten years
has fallen behind the increase in business to be done
by the railways, an adequate impression may be
obtained of the imminence of the dangers and the
magnitude of the practical problems to be found on
the financial side of the transportation question.

CHAPTER XIV

The Railroad

PART III — LEGISLATIVE REGULATION AND ITS LIMITS

THE fundamental principles of construction, operation, financing and ratemaking have been stated in the last two chapters. There remains to be considered the nature and amount of control exercised by the public in one way or another over the direction and detail of railroad affairs. The ramifications of the transportation interest are so extensive, the matter so directly affects every citizen of the country, and it has been for so many years thrust constantly to the front in public discussion and political campaigns that some consideration of the legislative regulation of railroads and its proper limits should have place in a statement of first principles.

First, emphasis should be laid on the fact that both the people and the railways lose by the folly and profit by the wisdom of either. There is no other partnership so intimate and indissoluble; because it is grounded not in the inclination of either, but in the nature of human society and the necessity of economic law. The public and the railroad must always prosper or suffer together. If the railroad's profits are too high, its patrons are impoverished. If they are too low, deficient service and a general decline in business and prosperity will follow. The carrier can provide an adequate service and maintain it at the point of highest efficiency, and the public can enjoy the benefits of that ideal condition only when there is a fair and just balance held between them. How to secure this is the pith of what is commonly called "the railroad problem."

The relation of the railway to the state — just where public control shall begin and how far it shall extend — has filled with dissension the last thirty years. Between the demand of some of the earlier railway corporations, that they should be substantially exempt from all regulation, and the demand made to-day that legislatures and commissions should have the right, without appeal, to order successive reductions in rates and increases in expense until the railways become bankrupt, there is somewhere a reasonable middle ground of justice. In trying to arrive at this through the American method of advance by the conflict of extremes, the railway properties of this country have passed through strange vicissitudes. It has been like the slow rise of water behind a dam, the sudden sweeping away of all restraints, and then a slow rebuilding on the old foundations with a larger knowledge bought by costly experience. One fixed correspondence, however, must be noted. The years in which the largest number of miles of railroad were built have been the years of greatest general prosperity.

The first radical exercise of a public control of rates

was followed by the evil years succeeding 1872. Then came a period of reorganization, placing the railroad once more on a sound basis and facing fairly the new conditions. In 1887 came the definite assertion and exercise of control by Congress, expressed in the Interstate Commerce Act. As originally enacted this proved neither unreasonable nor hurtful. It did not deny the right of the railway to earn a living. And its enforcement did not injure the credit or prevent the expansion of the railroads, because it proved that, in the main, they were dealing fairly with the public. The late Joseph Nimmo, Jr., has stated that, of 9,099 complaints entertained by the Commission during the first eighteen years of its existence, 9,054 were settled directly, without reference to the courts, forty-five only of the remaining cases were appealed to the courts, and of these only eight were sustained. All of these cases alleged unjust discrimination and not one asserted an exorbitant rate. It is estimated that the total freight transactions to which the railroads of the United States were a party amounted during the same period to nearly three billions. With an open tribunal established for this particular class of grievances, the complaints were fewer than one in three hundred thousand. In these billions of transactions, eight only were censured by the courts. The figures are eloquent of the observance of law by the railroad interest.

But the matter did not end here. Subsequent legislation proposed to vest practical control and management of these properties in an outside body, politically appointed. Rapidly an era of frenzied legislation against the railroads drew on. Many of the states, incited by consciousness of their power and by every art of which the demagogue is master, proceeded to devote themselves for some years almost wholly to railroad-baiting. Within three years, ending in 1907, twenty-five states enacted car-service laws, twenty-three regulated train service and connections, twenty-two fixed maximum passenger rates, nine enacted maximum freight rates, thirty-six regulated the general corporate affairs of common carriers. In five years of the same period fifteen state railroad commissions were created or received large extensions of power. Thirty-three states enacted a total of 334 laws regulating railroads within their jurisdiction, and nearly all these laws were passed without proper investigation or knowledge of their probable effect.

These facts are some measure of the violence of the attack upon the railway interest; nearly every item of which had for its moving purpose or included as one of its results the decrease of railroad revenue or the increase of operating expense, or both. Rates were cut by arbitrary edict to a minimum unjustified by traffic conditions and incompatible with operation except at a loss. For it has already been seen that efficiency is nearing its maximum. The railroads cannot be crowded much further. The weight of rails, the capacity of cars, the power of locomotives all have a practical limit that cannot be exceeded in the pursuit of new economies to meet new impositions;

and that limit has nearly or quite been reached. Every department of the railroad business was invaded by the doctrinaire and the demagogue, as well as the sincere legislator handicapped by ignorance of the practical side of the great interest with which he was attempting to deal. Hours of labour were shortened, changes in construction and rolling stock costing hundreds of millions were ordered, and the law, while forbidding combination, at the same time made competition impossible by prohibiting discrimination, insisting upon a minimum rate and standardizing the main conditions of the business. While imposing these new burdens, the public kept demanding special rates for special occasions, including innumerable conventions and similar gatherings; and turned first, as usual, to the railroads with assurance when money contributions were desired for some public purpose.

The consequences of this attitude of fierce unreason became acute in the fall of 1907. The confidence of the public in the security and prosperity of the railroad business yielded finally to continuous legislative attack. The Interstate Commerce Commission's Report for 1897, after most of the reorganizing work had been done, had shown that more than 70 per cent. of the entire outstanding stock of the railroads of the country paid no dividends, and 16.59 per cent. of their bonds, exclusive of equipment trust obligations, paid no interest whatever. Yet ten years later an additional burden of some twenty million dollars a year was imposed on the railways by new regulative measures that did not add a dollar to their income. As a consequence of this continuous policy of drastic measures, the value of securities alone fell off nearly five billion dollars, while business credits decreased in probably equal volume. Had it not been for sound industrial conditions underneath, the country would not have recovered from the shock for twenty years.

Not since 1893 had there been any such list of railroad wreckages as occurred in 1908. During that year over 8,000 miles of road passed into the hands of receivers; while crippled operation and injured credit represented greater damage than statistics can express. Half a million railway employees lost their employment, directly or indirectly. A part of the decline in treasury receipts is the price the public pays for the legislative persecution of railroads that culminated in 1907. They were saved from total destruction only by the protection that the courts, under the Constitution, give to property against confiscation. But complete recovery is a slow process, and can be looked for only after some authoritative assurance that such assaults are ended.

No public question touches directly the interests of so large a number of people, especially those who work hard for a living, as the prosperity of the railroads and their subordination to proper and freedom from improper regulation. The railroad has been an emancipator of labour. A commodity brings the highest price when it can move quickly to any point where demand may arise. This is notably true of labour.

Its employment and wages depend upon freedom of movement from place to place. Therefore the rise of the national transportation system has meant much not only to the farmer whose products it brings to market, and to its own employees who now outnumber those of any other employer, but to every artisan, factory hand and other worker in the country. A considerable part of the United States would be literally uninhabitable without railroads. Climatic conditions would make life insupportable to any large population if comforts and necessaries could not be brought in from a distance. Some of the systems serving such territory have already been reduced by oppressive legislation to a financial condition so precarious that their service breaks down whenever subjected to any unusual strain; such, for instance, as a severe winter brings to the carrier. Business is injured or paralyzed; and the very lives of the people may be endangered by a policy which may in any emergency put before a railroad the choice between making its service insufficient, or even partially discontinuing it, and inviting virtual bankruptcy. This negative fact is the complement of the still more impressive positive fact that not the growth of manufactures or the general conditions which we call progress or the increase of humanity or the rise of labour unions has done so much to better the condition and broaden the opportunity for labour as has the railroad.

This being true, it is singular that the public should be willing to mulct a railroad at every opportunity;

for the same public also in the long run pays all the bills. Yet this disposition appears not only in a huge volume of legislation reducing rates, but in new forms and higher rates of taxation, in the readiness of juries to give large verdicts in damage suits, in the indifference of public authorities generally to the injury or destruction of railroad property. Every dollar thus called for comes out of the pockets of the people. The railroad is practically helpless against unjust exactions. The people along its line may all move away if it suits them, but it must remain. It must do business with the community in which its lot is cast, and make a living. Even a receivership does not destroy track or equipment, which must still find occupation and get some equivalent for their service. The mere politician would not dare to attack and abuse any other interest as he does this, for it would remove to some locality where it could get fair play, and the community would be a heavy loser. Because the railroad cannot do this, fair-minded men should be not less but more inclined to insist that it receive everywhere, in the legislature, in the courts, in the forum of public opinion, the full measure of an equal and just consideration. Two things are self-evident: one, that it has not had this in the past; the other that, until it has been granted, there can be no permanent peace and prosperity in the world of industrial development or that of public affairs.

A railroad must earn money or borrow it. It has no other resource. The stockholder gets a dividend which is usually a fixed and very low figure on most of the big systems of the country. Increase expense, and the public, not the railroad, is taxed. The railroads of the United States paid out more money for taxes alone in the year 1908 than the total receipts of all the railroads of Australia and those of the government railroads of New Zealand and Canada combined. In the last twenty years this tax bill of our railroads has increased over 200 per cent. If this came from some private hoard, if it were like an inheritance tax or an extra charge on luxuries consumed by a few individuals, it would still, when compared with the increase in other taxation, prove persecution.

In 1907 the total taxes paid by the railways of the United States were nearly 10 per cent. of their net earnings from operation. For 1908 the percentage is about 12. This is, in effect, an income tax. The proposal to raise the income tax in England from 5 to 7½ per cent. is considered so revolutionary that the whole country is aflame with the issue. In no other country, and upon no other form of industry or investment in this, are such unreasonable imposts laid. When railroad property is assessed for taxing purposes, the public insists that it is never valued high enough; when the value of the property as an element in rate-making is in question, the same public insists that it is never made low enough. The inconsistency of the prevailing attitude toward the railroad is as marked as is its injustice. The owner of every other form of property may enjoy without reproach its natural increase; but if a railroad's property gains value, this is considered proper ground for legislative attack. Representing as railroad taxation does an extra burden placed by the people through the politicians on their own backs, its enormous increase and its methods prove to how slight an extent reason and intelligent self-interest have as yet been applied to the details of the relation between the railroad and the public. The assertion of their identity of interest is only the expression of an economic fact as certain and universal as the influence of gravitation. Perpetual conflict between them is not so much civil war as suicide.

Although the tendency to interfere unnecessarily and hurtfully with the management of railroad properties has by no means been killed, its virulence has been somewhat abated by recent disastrous experiences. There will always be railroad regulation. But railroad persecution shows symptoms of ptomaine poisoning. Its excesses generated toxins which are destroying its power to harm; and the country may probably look forward presently to a period of constructive legislation, after the destructive period that ended its reign of more than a quarter of a century in 1907.

The relation of public authority to the railroad hereafter should be and probably will be more supervisory than prescriptive. No arbiter not familiar with the whole situation, as only railway officials themselves can be, is qualified to fix the details of operation or to decide questions that may, notwithstanding apparent simplicity, involve the ruin of a corporation on the one hand or of a community on the other. Reasonable men, especially those who have had business experience, realize that the state may and must stand in the background as a judicial referee and an enforcing executive. Its part is to correct ascertained evils, and to see that the regulations which it finds necessary to lay down are observed. Mr. Henry S. Haines, in his recent book on the subject, expresses the following conclusion, which harmonizes with economic principles and practical common sense:

"Our national wealth is largely invested in property which, though productive, is not readily convertible. The world elsewhere is demanding the means to develope unutilized resources of nature, and that wealth which is not attached to the soil may flit away to lands where it may be more profitably employed. Let us, then, not legislate against the railroads, but for them! Let us regard the ills of which we complain as not inherent in the application of private capital to public use, but as incidental to the unrestricted control of concentrated capital; and let us seek the remedy which will restrict that control to purposes consistent with the public welfare, with powers so clearly defined as to be unmistakable in their limitations, and with such efficient supervision as will insure publicity in the exercise of corporate authority. Surely such a remedy can be found in legislation which will not be so drastic as to also limit the legitimate profits upon private capital invested in the railroad corporations engaged in the performance of a public service."

There should be a few laws, thoroughly enforced. The attempt to prescribe details for so vast and complicated an undertaking must necessarily end in failure. It follows that the tendency of late years has been more and more to substitute Federal for state regulation. Forty-six different authorities cannot issue orders separately to a single interest without endless confusion and contradictions. There can be but one final authority over the railroads. No subject can serve two masters, and much less forty-six. The greater cannot be included in the less; nor the interstate traffic, which constitutes from 65 to 97 per cent. of the total over large areas of the country, accept directions from the comparatively trifling volume of business that originates and ends within the boundaries of a single state.

Regulative authority there must be. But it must be consistent, comprehensive and uniform. It must be governed by the rule of fair play to the shipper, the railroad and the consumer alike. Behind ruthless aggression by either corporation or state stands the menacing figure of public ownership. This has no power to affright the present owners of railroads, since their property could not be taken without fair compensation. But for the people it would be the beginning of the end. No sane man can believe that our institutions or free government in this country would long survive the change.

No government could or would have effected any such reduction of rates as has taken place in the last thirty years. Public control is everywhere slow, inefficient, expensive. There is not a department of our Federal government in which private initiative and modern business methods would not insure greater expedition, better results and a saving in cost of from 25 to 50 per cent. Our own experience in other respects and the experience of state-owned railroads everywhere, when their finances are carefully examined and honestly stated, show that government ownership would require a material and probably a regularly advancing increase in railroad rates.

Government operation of railroads would necessarily establish the uniform rule of a distance tariff; not only to satisfy the clamours and complaints of different communities, but to comply with the requirements of the Constitution and the rule that there shall be no discrimination. Nothing could throw transportation at its present stage of development into more inextricable confusion, destroy many important business centres more surely or more increase the cost of carriage on main commodities of commerce and main lines of travel than a distance tariff.

In this connection it is significant that, since legislative regulation became the order of the day, especially that by Act of Congress, none of the small towns of the country have shown marked growth. The large centres have gained, because they are necessarily the basing points for making rates. This gives them a business advantage. The smaller centres have, so far as their hoped-for commercial importance is concerned, been wiped out. The effect of Federal regulation here, as in the case of destroying competition by compelling the adoption of standard rates, has been the exact opposite of what was intended and expected. Its extension will be marked by a still further aggrandizement of the few large strategic traffic centres at the expense of all smaller cities and towns.

Aside from all economic questions, Federal ownership would mean the political appointment of an army of employees now in excess of sixteen hundred thousand, and soon to number two millions, mostly thoroughly organized and ready to act as a unit in whatever direction their own interests may dictate. Every man who does not wilfully blind himself to consequences must admit that our institutions could not stand the strain; and that the establishment of Federal ownership of railroad properties would mean the destruction of free government in the United States.

Happily, signs that reason is resuming her sway are not wanting. While propositions are still heard in some quarters for railroad legislation that cannot be justified either by economic principle or existing fact, they are listened to with less approval and pressed with less avidity. The people have learned something of their own interest as inseparable from fair treatment of their common carriers. Soon after the railroad came, the wealth of the United States was estimated, in 1850, at about $7,000,000,000. It is now estimated at more than $130,000,000,000. More than any other single agency, the railroad is to be credited with this wonderful increase. The public is coming to understand that it must not be destroyed.

The railway system of this country is not a failure, as has been charged by men who are without knowledge of the facts, and whose opinion consequently is of no value. On the contrary, it is, when judged by its results, in official records, perhaps the most conspicuous success achieved in the development of the United States. Costing only from one-half to one-fifth as much as the systems of other countries, it charges rates from one-third to one-half as great and pays over twice the rate of wages. Few inventions produced by American genius, probably no other industry perfected by American enterprise, can show a record that compares with this. The railroad men of this country have a right to resent the indiscriminate abuse too common in the past, and the railroad interest has a right to demand the protection of the laws and the support of an intelligent and righteous public opinion. Just as there is no better measure of the overflowing energy and unconquerable determination of the American people than the upbuilding of this mighty system in the face of great obstacles, so will there be no fitter test of their capacity for self-government than their ability to hold the scales of justice fairly balanced between the conduct of our railway systems and the supervisory and regulative authority of the state.

What goes by the name of "the railroad problem" will be solved at the same time and by the same method as the other problems of conduct and ethics inherent in all human social relations. The duty of the good citizen toward the railway is to insist that it shall be

punished when it does wrong, and protected in possession and enjoyment of its property and in the
performance of its public functions when it is right.
Vindictiveness in either direction is worthy only of
the savage or the brigand. The people must remember
here as everywhere else, if they do not wish to end in
colossal failure, that the very first condition laid down
in the preamble to the Constitution of the United
States, after united effort, as preliminary to the formation of any government worthy of the name, is — "to
establish justice."

Give the railroads a square deal and allow them to
earn a fair return on their value. Compel them
to do the work that they can do and are intended to
do for a compensation reasonable when viewed from
both sides. Make them render a fair service for a fair
price, and permit them to earn and keep a fair income.
If this rule could be the ideal of the American people,
instead of a gospel of abuse and hate, it would not only
close equitably an agitation disastrous to both parties,
but it would result practically in the establishment at
an early day of traffic conditions more favourable to
the public than it has ever known.

It is time for the whole country to sober down and
think out the issues before it. They are serious enough
to demand its most earnest effort. They are vital
enough to elicit the most generous patriotism. This
country has become the most prosperous in the world
not by any magic of legislation, but by the coöperation
of all its people in the development of natural resources

more abundant than were ever before placed at the command of any people. Constructive statesmanship must now re-establish and confirm disturbed relations between the activities engaged in the production of national wealth. A hearty union of all interests, a broad and genuine understanding and a deliberate, honest and tolerant attitude on the part of the people will do most to promote success in industry and sanity and permanence in the nation.

CHAPTER XV

The Conservation of Capital

AT a meeting of the Minnesota Agricultural Society in 1906, I called attention to the waste of our national resources and to the choice between facing about and inviting national disaster. At the time, this warning was less seriously received at home, perhaps, than in European countries, where it was widely circulated and discussed. But the sober second thought of our own people soon lifted the subject to its proper place, and conservation is now a watchword not only for the nation but for the several states. The public is beginning to understand and sympathize with the broader view that sees national resources, industries and interests closely related to and dependent upon one another. How rapidly and how far the movement has travelled and its scope extended is shown by the resolution adopted by the National Conservation Congress as its creed, and the schedule of subjects drawn up by its committee.

The resolution reads: "Resolved, That the objects of this congress shall be broad, to act as a clearing house for all allied social forces of our time, to seek to overcome waste in natural, human or moral forces." The programme of topics for debate and report included lands, irrigation, navigation, water powers, flood waters, forests, minerals and other resources. Such is the width of vision and interpretation of the conservation interest to-day. But there is one subject missing; and it is the second in importance of them all. Next after the conservation of the land, its area, use and fertility, must come the conservation of national capital, in the shape of cash and credit.

Experience has shown how surely prosperity follows the right employment and misfortune the abuse of this great national resource. Yet in the schedules of proposed conservation activity the waste of national power through excessive expenditure and overburdening of credit has apparently been overlooked. This forgotten item must be added to the list. The friends of conservation should take steps everywhere to give to this indispensable possession the same protection from the spoiler that they are trying to give to the soil, the forest, the water power and deposits of mineral wealth.

We are living in an age of world-wide financial delirium. Most nations have thrown away moderation in the spending of money. A couple of centuries ago, when a monarch wanted money for his pleasures or his schemes of aggrandizement, he had to place a new tax on windows or chimneys or salt or some other object such that the people felt the pressure immediately. Both were warned in time; and before the process could go too far, either protest or revolution attempted to remedy the evil. Modern conditions are totally different. The immense increase of wealth all over the world has greatly augmented the supply of capital. The mobility of this capital, the ease by which through international exchanges it can be made to satisfy a need now in one country and now in another, strengthens the impression that it is inexhaustible.

Take France, which is able to finance almost anything from a war to a manufacturing enterprise in any part of the world. Leroy-Beaulieu estimates that the wealth of the French people increases by about a billion dollars every year. This increment may be drawn upon by enterprise anywhere. It is not gathered in huge fortunes, but is distributed among millions of holders in small sums of a few thousand francs each. These are collected by the great banking concerns, ready for employment on good security in any quarter of the globe. While France is the best saver, she is not the richest of the nations. The average wealth per capita in some other countries is higher. The per capita wealth in the United States shows the following changes in the last sixty years:

1850	$ 307.69
1860	513 93
1870	779.83
1880	870 20
1890	1,035.57
1900	1,164 79
1904	1,318.11

Undoubtedly, at the present scale of prices, the per capita wealth of the United States to-day is well over

$1,500. In most other nations the growth, while not so rapid, has been steady and substantial. The addition of these uncounted billions to the aggregate wealth of the world has stimulated the spirit of financial adventure and the love of squandering inherent in mankind. Its availability has lulled to sleep natural prudence and quieted the alarm of moments of sanity in the spendthrift's life; with what results will presently be seen.

If credit has, as Daniel Webster said, done more than all the mines of the world to develop and increase its industry, the potential dangers of credit are equally great. Expansion or contraction of cash is measured by millions; of credits, by billions. The increase of apparent resources by an easy resort to borrowing, the mortgaging of a patrimony not our own to obtain material for present extravagance, the diversion of wealth from productive to unproductive uses — all these have gone further than most people realize. It will be worth while to examine current public waste of cash and credit. It is measured by current debt and current expenditure everywhere, as compared with the same items only a few years ago.

The people of the United States inherited from its founders a wholesome tradition against debt, which is only now disappearing from the conduct of national affairs. This, together with the enormous resources at our command and the consequent ability of our people to pay increasing taxes without distress, has kept our national debt at a moderate figure. Until the time of the Spanish War and the Panama Canal, it decreased. It now tends to rise, concealed under the polite fiction of certificates of indebtedness to cover treasury deficits. If the advocates of large bond issues for all manner of internal improvements should carry their point, if that resource is not definitely restricted to the emergency of war, we will be in the condition of Europe, where the motto of every chancellory now seems to be: "After us the deluge."

The following figures give the estimated total of the national debts of the countries of Europe at different dates. Where statistics cover so wide a field there may be some inaccuracies of detail; but, in the great aggregate, these are of no practical consequence:

1785–89	$2,070,600,000
1814–18	7,213,800,000
1845–48	7,967,000,000
1874	18,027,800,000
1905–07	29,552,800,000

These are not statistics of expenditure, but of debt. After raising from their people by taxation all they can be made to contribute without dangerous unrest, the balance of money spent by these governments increased by twenty-seven and a half billion dollars in one hundred and twenty years. It increased eleven and one-half billions, or more than 60 per cent., in the last thirty years. The annual interest charge of Europe is now over $1,200,000,000 a year. She is in the position of a debtor who must constantly add to the principal of his obligations in order to get money to keep him from defaulting on the interest.

The new budget threatens to shake the political foundations of England with its revolutionary proposals for raising more money, where borrowing had become impossible without turmoil and another drop in the price of consols. Germany has been issuing treasury bills for years to cover deficits. The debt of the empire and the several states combined is over $4,000,000,000. The other nations of Europe are mostly travelling the same road. Now how about ourselves?

Leaving out the debts of counties, municipalities and school districts, the aggregate debt of all the states and territories, less sinking fund assets, was $274,745,772 in 1880; in 1890 it was $211,210,487; and in 1902 it was $234,908,873. The decrease for the first decade was 23.1 per cent.; and the increase for the twelve-year period to 1902 was 11.2 per cent. Inasmuch as there was in the former a readjustment of debts in many states by scaling down the principal, a fair comparison on equal terms would probably show that the actual burden of debt on the states only is growing slowly but with a tendency to accelerate its movement.

Very different is the showing when the obligations of counties and other minor civil divisions are included. In our cities modern extravagance finds its most untrammeled expression. The total debt of the states, including all these minor civil divisions, increased $13,921,443, or 1.25 per cent., between 1880 and 1890.

Between 1890 and 1902 it increased $727,778,393, or 64 per cent. Nearly three-quarters of a billion in twelve years, an average increase of $60,000,000 a year in the amount borrowed by the people, ought to make any country stop and think. Most of the actual material development is privately financed, and carries its own bonded indebtedness, which the public finances cannot take into account. The figures down to 1910, outside of and in addition to the national debt, would probably show an increase of a billion and a quarter to a billion and a half dollars for the last twenty years, and a grand total of over two and a quarter billion dollars; about double what it was in 1890.

Debt figures, however, do not begin to tell the story of our national extravagance. Only a small part of our public expenditure is represented by debt tables. The rest is raised by increased taxation. In part this consists of new imposts, new licenses and fees; and in part it comes from increased assessments of all property, that provide more revenue without showing an increased tax-rate. Nothing bears more directly or forcibly upon the subject of national waste and the conservation of national resources than the profligacy disclosed by our public expense ledgers. Every figure that follows has been taken from official records, or is the result of compiling their contents in summaries never before presented to the public.

First, as to the nation. For the United States Government the official statements cover only what are known as "net ordinary disbursements." This

total does not include the whole of the disbursements
for the postal service, or any payment on the principal
of the public debt, or those extraordinary expenses
that cut an ever-increasing figure in national finances.
It covers mostly routine charges, and therefore falls
short each year of the actual appropriations made by
Congress for that year. Taken alone, figures so far
under the fact would be misleading. Relatively they
are sufficient for the purpose, since they vary with
our general policy. A comparison of the net ordinary
expenditures by decades will show the trend of national
spending. The amounts are as follows:

1870	$293,657,005
1880	264,847,637
1890	297,736,487
1900	487,713,792
1908	659,196,320

Although the great business expansion of this
country began right after the Civil War, the expenses
for 1890 were but four million dollars greater than
those of twenty years before. Since 1890 these expenditures have grown by $180,000,000 each nine years on
the average, or $20,000,000 a year, until now they
are 121.4 per cent. more than they were eighteen years
ago. Expressed in terms of per capita outgo, these
charges, which are only part of the cost of maintaining
the Federal Government, rose from $4.75 in 1890 to
$6.39 in 1900, and to $7.56 in 1908.

Shift the focus of the glass a little closer and look at

our states and cities. By official records the total
expenditure of state government alone in all the states
and territories of the Union combined was $77,105,911
in 1890, and $185,764,202 in 1902. The increase in
these twelve years was $108,658,291, or 141 per cent.
The aggregate expenditures of all the states, together
with their minor civil divisions of counties, municipalities and school districts, rose from $569,252,634 in
1890 to $1,156,447,085 in 1902. The increase was
$587,194,451, or 103 per cent. Expressed in per
capita terms, this means that the cost of state government only was $1.24 for each person in 1890 and $2.35
in 1902; for states and minor civil divisions combined
it was $9.09 in 1890 and $14.64 in 1902. A few
exercises in compound proportion will show what it
may be twenty or thirty years hence.

Official figures from 1880 to 1909 have been obtained
from thirty of the states, covering all New England;
New York, New Jersey and Pennsylvania of the mid-
Atlantic section; all the representative commonwealths
of the rich Middle West and Northwest; and a sprink-
ling of the states of the South and the extreme West.
These, including as they do two-thirds in number,
four-fifths of the population and the great bulk of the
wealth of the whole country, will show whether or
not local extravagance is still spreading its wings.
The aggregate expenditure of these states, not including their counties or municipalities, increased 28.6
per cent. between 1880 and 1890; 58 per cent. between
1890 and 1900; 90.7 per cent. between 1900 and 1909.

Expressed in per capita terms, the cost of government in these thirty states was $1.78 for each individual in 1880; $1.79 in 1890; $2.35 in 1900; and, assuming the same rate of growth in population as in previous years, according to the government estimate, $3.84 in 1909. All these different series of statistical facts, traced independently, confirm and reinforce one another.

It is always asserted, when the truth is told and a demand for economy is made, that the development of the country and its increase of wealth have been so great as both to require and justify this enlarged outlay. The answer to the charge of a billion dollar session of Congress is that this has become a billion dollar country. The apology is neither relevant nor true. It is not necessary that expense should increase in the same ratio as growth. But the growth of expenditure has so far outrun the growth of the country that the actual figures are almost incredible. The following little table, exhibiting the whole situation, might be printed at the top of every letterhead used by any man in public office anywhere in the United States:

INCREASES

Wealth	1870	to	1890	116%	1890 to 1904	65%
Foreign Trade	"	"	"	99%	" " 1908	85.4%
Value Manufactured Prod.	"	"	"	121%	" " 1905	58%
Net Ordinary Exp. U. S. Gov't	"	"	"	1.4%	" " 1908	121.4%
Expenditures 30 States .					" " 1909	201.6%

The moral of these half-dozen lines is overwhelming and their proof of public waste is complete. The rate

of development of the country was far more rapid in
the twenty years from 1870 to 1890 than it was in the
eighteen from 1900 to 1908. Yet in the earlier era,
when every great national asset was doubled in twenty
years and the pressure for enlarged activities was correspondingly severe upon the state, the net ordinary
expenditures of the United States increased but 1.4
per cent. If it is national growth that makes government costly, how about this period? Since then,
with a commercial expansion expressed by a much
smaller percentage, these net ordinary expenses have
jumped over 121 per cent. The wealth and business
of the country as a whole increased but little more
than half as fast in the second period as in the first.
The expenses of the Federal Government increased 88
times as fast, and the expenses of the state governments in the last nineteen years went up over 200 per
cent. By such facts as these, quite as convicting as
slaughtered forests or exhausted mines or impoverished
soils or appropriated water powers, two things are
settled once for all: no honest man should ever again
adduce material development as a sufficient reason
for the growing appropriation bills of nation or state;
and the conservation movement should give to economy in national, state and municipal expenditure
a leading place on its programmes, and a share of
effort commensurate with its importance and the
country's need.

The phenomenal increase of public expenditure
has already produced a plentiful crop of public ills.

It is one of the causes of the increase in prices now disturbing the people. This increase follows in a suggestive way the inflation of national and local budgets. The average cost of the supplies that must be bought for practically every household has increased about 50 per cent. between 1896 and 1909. During the past year there has been a marked lifting of the price level. Foodstuffs cost from 10 to 70 per cent. more than ten years ago. Inquiries are now under way which, when fairly and intelligently carried out, will give some accurate measure of the extent and force of the movement of prices. The reports of the Federal Bureau of Labor show that, if we represent the average prices of the ten years 1890–1899 by 100, the price of food in 1908 was 120.6; of clothing, 116.9; of fuel and lighting, 130.8; of metals and implements, 125.4; of lumber and building materials, 133.1; and of all commodities combined, 122.8. These are wholesale prices. If to them be added the profit of the retailer, a fairly good idea can be formed of the new conditions of our national life.

The man who attempts to place entire responsibility for these changes upon one single act or influence lacks either fairness or intelligence. As in most great economic movements, the cause is complex. Something is due to enormous currency inflation. The total per capita circulation in the United States in 1896 was $21.41, and in 1909 it was $35.01. Although population had grown by many millions in these thirteen years, the amount of money to each individual had increased by $13.60, or more than 60 per cent. The increase in the total gold production of the world, which rose from $118,848,000 in 1890 to over $427,000,000 in 1908 has been made the basis for one form and another of credit issues aggregating a vast sum. Even a rudimentary knowledge of economics or monetary science shows that such changes must produce a rise of prices.

The tariff is another contributing cause. It is true that it can furnish but a partial explanation. For to only a limited extent can the rise in food prices be affected by or traced to the tariff. As to commodities that we export, the tariff is inoperative. It generally affects prices directly as we become importers. Nevertheless the tariff must bear its share of responsibility for rising prices. Common sense says that, when the cost of the necessaries of life in a town on the Canadian side of the Detroit River is reported at nearly 25 per cent. less than on the American side, the tariff accounts for the difference. It says that a man will raise his charges to the full extent that he is guaranteed against competition. He who believes that the sudden and violent rise of prices in 1897, following the enactment of the Dingley law, and the similar movement following the passage of the tariff act of 1909 have no relation to those legislative achievements would argue that the rise of the Seine had nothing to do with the recent inundation of Paris.

Combinations which are actually in restraint of trade, which have monopolized their field and are either controlled by a common secret management or a secret agreement to maintain exorbitant charges are partly responsible. If the operations of these had been followed with the same interest by the public and checked with the same vigour by state and nation that are displayed in agitation against the railroads which for years have been subject to public control, open to public inspection, and which, practically alone among the agencies affecting directly the common life, have given their services at lower and lower prices every decade, the country would not be so stupefied as it is to-day by a great hardship or so bewildered about the remedy.

Still more of the rise of prices is due to the failure of agricultural production to keep up with the increase of population. Taking the average for five-year periods, it was shown in the chapter on "Farm Methods" that the wheat crop of the country increased 41 per cent. in the twenty-five years ended in 1908. From 1880 the population increased 74 per cent. The decrease in wheat exports was 24 per cent. When wheat sold at sixty-five cents per bushel, it was because the world's product was relatively in excess of the world's demand. The ratio is now reversed, and demand, taking the world as a whole, is gaining on supply. And this is particularly true of the United States, with its rapid increase in population, its drift to the cities and its consequent actual falling off in important items of food products. Between January 1, 1909, and January 1, 1910, the number of cattle other than milch cows in this country decreased by more than 2,000,000, following a decrease of 700,000 the year before. The number of swine decreased 6,365,000, on top of a decrease of nearly 2,000,000 the year before. The number of mouths to be fed is always increasing. These are conditions under which a simple exercise in division proves the necessity of price advances. It was definitely shown in advance that they must come.

When due allowance has been made for the effect of these forces that make for dearer living, there still remains a large unexplained balance. This must be credited to the lavish expenditure which has now grown to be a national trait, which is eating up our accumulated wealth, and which is forcing prices higher and higher by consuming our resources unproductively, encouraging indolence and luxury, and compelling resort to a constantly ascending scale of wages. With these three powerful economic forces converging upon the price average, the country could no more escape the corresponding rise and no more cure it than a man could keep the mercury from rising in the tube of a thermometer while he was holding a burning glass so as to focus the blaze of the sun upon its bulb. This is the full meaning of the somewhat widely quoted statement made by me, that it is not so much the high cost of living as the cost of high living that afflicts the country.

Waste, idleness and rising wages, all inter-related with one another, now as cause and now as effect, are, next to an over-issue of irredeemable paper, the three most powerful forces in the world to raise prices. First, waste. This is shown in the federal, state and municipal expense bills already exhibited. There has been mild objection in Washington to the demand of a certain investigating body for an appropriation of a quarter of a million dollars to pursue inquiries on which it had already spent $651,000 without any practical results. A charge of over $7,000,000 a year for secret service, an appanage of dictators and abhorred by every really free democracy, awakened a certain amount of criticism. In every state there have been created within the last thirty years dozens or scores of commissions, boards, officials, posts, all with salaries attached, all asking for more and all heaping up incidental expenses. Billions of free capital have been absorbed by the great wars of recent times, and by such disasters as visited San Francisco, Southern Italy and Paris. We are spending some hundreds of millions at Panama, and the aim of legislators ambitious of popularity is to find new vents for the treasury. Capital in untold volume has been withdrawn by all these policies from productive employments. Now we cannot cheat the first four rules of arithmetic. We cannot spend money for one thing and also use it for another. The same money that has bought an automobile is not on hand to build a steam thresher. There has been less capital for production; hence less production; hence a diminished supply; hence higher prices.

Second, habits of idleness thus encouraged diminish

production. Where so much public money is flowing down the gutter, many a man finds it easier to scoop up what he wants than to work for it. The fashion of public extravagance is of all fashions the first and most easily imitated. As the supply of capital dwindles on the one side of the economic machine, the supply of labour dwindles on the other. We must expect to see this also reflected in higher prices. And so long as the world has to live by labour, there will be no escape from and no exception to this law.

Third, perhaps the greatest factor of all in the price problem is the wage rate. Everybody knows that labour cost is the principal item in all forms of industry. The wage rate has been rising steadily in this country. Powerful forces are back of this movement. It has public sympathy. To resist it is difficult and may be dangerous. As the labour supply diminishes, for reasons just stated, wages rise still more. High wages and high prices work in a circle. Every rise of one is reflected in a rise of the other. But somebody has to pay these wages. They do not come out of the air. In the end labour suffers when the business no longer pays a profit and the payrolls cease entirely by the closing up of an industry no longer profitable.

As cost of production is chiefly labour cost, the price of the finished article must go up if the price of labour is raised. This is just as true of the farm as of the factory. And the wages of farm labour have risen with the wages of labour in the trades. The complaint of every farmer who has to hire help is that farm labourers are both scarce and expensive. The fact that tea, coffee, sugar and such commodities, which are mainly imported, have risen little or none while other prices were soaring indicates that the high American wage rate raises prices and keeps them high. Since the labourer must receive for his work such compensation as will supply him with the necessaries of life at whatever market price they command, his wages must rise with every rise in the cost of living.

The effect of national waste of capital is felt immediately in the added weight of taxation. One of the last things men learn is that every dollar paid out by a government must first have been paid in by the community. The income raised by any tax save those on articles of pure luxury is so much taken from productive industry; and, where not utilized for public protection, in that narrow range of activity which alone is either proper or profitable for the state, is as truly wasted as if it were spent on public games or childish bonfires. Logically, the progress of the tax-collector, the search for new objects and new methods of taxation and the exaltation of a tax into something beneficent in itself instead of a necessary evil have kept pace with the advance in national and local extravagance.

The taxes collected annually from the railroads of the country have increased, as shown in a previous chapter, more than 200 per cent. since 1889. They increased by forty million dollars and by more than $100 per mile of track between 1900 and 1908. Franchise taxes, in-heritance taxes, taxes on corporations and income taxes are all recent additions or suggestions. They are re-ferred to here with neither approval nor disapproval as means of collecting money, but as part of the evil pro-geny of our dissipation of free capital. Not only these but a host of others must be resorted to if we carry out all the schemes that are hatched in the hotbed of waste. The experience of England with her budget, of every Continental country groaning under heavy taxes, must become our own if our policy is not reversed. The effect upon industry, prosperity and national character of a constantly mounting tax-rate, with its withdrawal of larger and larger sums every year from the fund that should be devoted to industrial enterprises and to the reproduction of wealth, is just as certain as the effect of drawing checks upon a bank to an annually larger and larger percentage of the deposits made.

In this way, insidiously and without realization by the general public, often under the specious names of improvement and reform, capital is dissipated, dis-couraged and quietly abstracted from industry. In this way the volume of employment is greatly lessened, because there is less capital for payrolls. In this way high prices and high wages and high taxes may all work together for the impoverishment of a nation by exactly the same process that works impoverish-ment of its soil. The analogy between reckless waste of natural resources and of capital is so close, the necessity of conservation in the one direction as well as the other is so evident, that it is not easy to understand why the more thoughtful of our people did not long ago take steps to apply a corrective.

The modern theory that you can safely tax the wealthy is just as obnoxious as the mediæval theory that you can safely oppress or kill the poor. It is obnoxious not because wealth deserves special consideration, but because capital is the main-spring of all industry and material development; and, after you have devoted so much of it to the unproductive purposes that the state represents when it transcends its primary function as keeper of the peace and administrator of justice, there will be just so much less left to pay out in wages and devote to the creation of other wealth. It is a fixed fact, exactly as it is that when you subtract x from y something less than y must remain. Of course the labourer suffers even more than the capitalist. The countries in which such forms of taxation are being carried furthest are precisely those in which employment is scarce and precarious, and labour finds it necessary to lean more and more heavily each year upon the weakening arm of state and public charity. In fact the whole subject is several thousand years old; and it is as amazing to find modern legislatures mulling over it as it would be if they debated hotly the comparative advantages of the rack and the thumb-screw as instruments of torture. The conclusion of the whole matter is well summed up in a recent article by Mr. J. Ellis Barker in the *Fortnightly Review,* in words as apt for the United

States as they were for the British public to whom they were addressed:

"Modern British financial policy, popular and democratic financial policy, the policy of taxing the wealthy for the benefit of the masses, is not a new one. It was practised by the Athenian democracy in the time of Cleon, and it led to the economic decay of Athens. It was practised in ancient Rome, and it led to the economic decay of Rome. It was practised by the Spaniards who plundered and drove out the wealthy Moors, who in the Middle Ages had made Spain a flourishing and wealthy industrial country, and it led to the economic decay of Spain. Throughout antiquity and the Middle Ages we meet with examples of the policy of taxing the rich out of existence for the benefit of the poor, and ruin has invariably been the result of that popular and democratic policy."

So it has been throughout history; and so it will be with us unless we are wise enough to avoid the hoary rock on which are plainly inscribed the legends and the warnings of the nations that made shipwreck there. It is to that fate and to no other that the socialistic experiment and all the policies that lead up to and feed it — the policies which, directly or indirectly, are responsible for the major part of increased public expenditure — must inevitably drag any country.

The saving feature of the situation is that it is not complex, and that the remedy is not obscure. The laws of conservation are everywhere few and plain. As the way to resume specie payments was to resume, so the way to conserve capital is to quit wasting it. Material resources are conserved by taking steps to stop their destruction. Just so the wealth of the country, its capital, its credit, must be saved from the predatory poor as well as the predatory rich, but above all from the predatory politician. Nothing less is worthy of honest men or of a people living under a government of their own fashioning and control.

The ideal of intelligent economy must be restored; let the rule be that every dollar unprofitably spent marks a crime against posterity just as much as does the dissipation of material resources.

Expenditure must be reduced all along the line; since a comparison with twenty years ago shows that it might be cut in two without injury to any real interest.

Credit everywhere should be conserved by a sharp scrutiny of new bond issues. The nation should reserve them for the crisis of war. No state need ever borrow again if it is wisely and honestly governed. The city that has fifty years of corporate life behind it, or has found it necessary to refund any portion of its bonded debt instead of paying at maturity, should be slow to draw upon its credit or mortgage the lives of its children yet unborn.

Stop grafting, the offspring of public extravagance and the parent of civic decay; not only the gross form that robs treasuries, but the more subtle and dangerous species that infects the masses of the people themselves.

Individual and public economy; a just distinction between a high standard of comfort on one side and vulgar ostentation or criminal waste on the other; a check on income-wasting, debt creation and credit inflation — these are the essentials of the new and better conservation. The reform is so great, so indispensable, so linked to our moral as well as our material progress that it would seem to appeal to the heart and mind of every American and win his enthusiastic devotion until its last battle shall have been won. Patriotism and self-interest strike hands here for the protection of our homes and happiness from those most dangerous of all enemies, the foes within our own borders.

The conservation movement must include this in its programme. It must stand for the defense and economic utilization of a resource without whose painful accumulation through centuries our forests and our mines would still contribute little to comfort or progress, and our fields would still wait the plough; a resource which represents the concentrated efforts and pains and hopes of a mighty past — every act of self-sacrifice of the father for his child, every reward of labour told into the treasury of savings for the future, the pulse of the strong hearts and the strain of the mighty sinews of all the millions who now are in their graves and have handed down to us their sacred trust. Encircled by the impregnable barrier which such a comprehensive policy of conservation should erect about it, the future of this nation would be secure indeed.

CHAPTER XVI

The Natural Wealth of the Land and Its Conservation

IN THE movement of modern times, which has made the world commercially a small place and has produced a solidarity of the race such as never before existed, we have come to the point where we must to a certain extent regard the natural resources of this planet as a common asset, compare them with demands now made and likely to be made upon them, and study their judicious use. Commerce, wherever untrammelled, is wiping out boundaries and substituting the world relation of demand and supply for smaller systems of local economy. The changes of a single generation have brought the nations of the earth closer together than were the states of this Union at the close of the Civil War. If we fail to consider what we possess of wealth available for the uses of mankind, and to what extent we are wasting a national patrimony that can never be restored, we might be likened to the directors of a company who never examine a balance sheet.

The sum of resources is simple and fixed. From the sea, the mine, the forest and the soil must be gathered everything that can sustain the life of man. Upon the wealth that these supply must be conditioned forever, so far as we can know, not only his progress but his continued existence on earth. How stands the inventory of property for our own people? The resources of the sea furnish less than 5 per cent. of the food supply, and that is all. The forests of this country, the product of centuries of growth, are fast disappearing. The best estimates reckon our standing merchantable timber at less than 2,000,000,000,000 feet. Our annual cut is about 40,000,000,000 feet. The lumber cut rose from 18,000,000,000 feet in 1880 to 34,000,000,000 feet in 1905; that is, it nearly doubled in twenty-five years. We are now using annually 500 feet board measure of timber per capita, as against an average of sixty feet for all Europe. The New England supply is gone. The Northwest furnishes small growths that would have been rejected by the lumberman thirty years ago. The South has reached its maximum production and begins to decline. On the Pacific Coast only is there now any considerable body of merchantable standing timber. We are consuming yearly three or four times as much timber as forest growth restores. Our supply of some varieties will be practically exhausted in ten or twelve years; in the case of others, without reforesting, the present century will see the end. When will we take up in a practical and intelligent way the restoration of our forests?

Turning now to one of the only two remaining sources of wealth, the mine, we find it differing from the others in an important essential. It is incapable of restoration or recuperation. The mineral wealth stored in the earth can be used only once. When iron and coal are taken from the mine, they cannot be restored; and upon iron and coal our industrial civilization is built. When fuel and iron become scarce and high-priced, civilization, so far as we can now foresee, will suffer as man would suffer by the gradual withdrawal of the air he breathes.

The exhaustion of our coal supply is not in the indefinite future. The startling feature of our coal production is not so much the magnitude of the annual output as its rate of growth. For the decade ending in 1905 the total product was 2,832,402,746 tons, which is almost exactly one-half the total product previously mined in this country. For the year 1906 the output was 414,000,000 tons, an increase of 46 per cent. on the average annual yield of the ten years preceding. In 1907 our production reached 470,000,000 tons. Fifty years ago the annual per capita production was a little more than one-quarter of a ton. It is now about five tons. It is but eight years since we took the place of Great Britain as the leading coal-producing nation of the world, and already our product exceeds hers by over 43 per cent., and is 37 per cent. of the known production of the world. Estimates of coal deposits still remaining must necessarily be somewhat vague, but they are approximately near the mark. The best authorities do not rate them at much over 2,000,000,000,000 tons. If coal production continues to increase as it has in the last ninety years, the available supply will be greatly reduced by the close of the century. Before that time arrives, however, the use of lower grades and mines of greater depth will become necessary; making the product inferior in quality and higher in price. Already Great Britain's industries have felt the check from a similar cause, as shown in her higher cost of production. Our turn will begin probably within a generation or two from this time. Yet we still think nothing of consuming this priceless resource with the greatest possible speed. Our methods of mining are often wasteful; and we not only prohibit our industries from having recourse to the coal supplies of other countries, but actually pride ourselves upon becoming exporters of a prime necessity of life and an essential of civilization.

The iron industry tells a similar story. The total of iron ore mined in the United States doubles about once in seven years. It was less than 12,000,000 tons in 1893, over 24,000,000 tons in 1899, 47,750,000 tons in 1906 and over 52,000,000 tons in 1907. The rising place of iron in the world's life is the most impressive phenomenon of the last century. In 1850 the pig iron production of the United States amounted to 563,758 tons, or about fifty pounds per capita. Our production now is over 600 pounds per capita. We do not work a mine, build a house, weave a fabric, prepare a meal or cultivate an acre of ground under modern methods without the aid of iron. We turn out over 25,000,000 tons of pig iron every year, and the production for the first half of 1907 was at the rate of 27,000,000 tons. This is two and one-half times the product of Great Britain. It is nearly half the product of the whole world. And the supply of this most precious of all the metals is so far from inexhaustible that it seems as if iron and coal might be united in their disappearance from common life.

A few years ago a Swedish geologist prepared for his Government a report which stated that the entire supply of the iron ore in the United States would be exhausted within the present century. The United States Geological Survey declared this an overstatement; but here is the conclusion of its own report, after a careful examination of the question in the light of the best authorities. I quote the official published document: "Assuming that the demand for iron ore during the present century may range from 50,000,000 to 100,000,000 tons per year, the Lake Superior district would last for from twenty-five to fifty years more, if it supplied the entire United States. But counting on the known reserves elsewhere in the United States, the ore will last for a much longer period, though, of course, it must necessarily show a gradual but steady increase in value and in cost of mining, along with an equally steady decrease in grade." The most favourable view of the situation forces the conclusion that iron and coal will not be available for common use on anything like present terms by the end of this century;

and our industrial, social and political life must be readjusted to meet the strains imposed by new conditions. Yet we forbid to our consumers access to the stores of other countries, while we boast of our increased exports of that material for want of which one day the nation may be reduced to the last extremity.

We now turn to the only remaining resource of man upon this earth, which is the soil itself. How are we caring for that, and what possibilities does it hold out to the people of future support? We are only beginning to feel the pressure upon the land. The whole interior of this continent, aggregating more than 500,000,000 acres, has been occupied by settlers within the last fifty years. What is there left for the next fifty years? Excluding arid and irrigable areas, the latter limited by nature, and barely enough of which could be made habitable in each year to furnish a farm for each immigrant family, the case stands as follows: In 1906 the total unappropriated public lands in the United States consisted of 792,000,000 acres. Of this area the divisions of Alaska, Arizona, California, Colorado, Idaho, Montana, Nevada, New Mexico and Wyoming contained 195,700,000 acres of surveyed and 509,000,000 acres of unsurveyed land. Little of Alaska is fitted for general agriculture, while practically all of the rest is semi-arid land, available only for grazing or irrigation. We have, subtracting these totals, 50,000,000 acres of surveyed and 36,500,000 acres of unsurveyed land as our actual remaining stock. And 21,000,000 acres were disposed of in

1907. How long will the remainder last? No longer can we say that "Uncle Sam has land enough to give us all a farm."

Equally threatening is the change in quality. There are two ways in which the productive power of the earth is lessened: first, by erosion and the sweeping away of the fertile surface into streams and thence to the sea; and, second, by exhaustion through wrong methods of cultivation. The former process has gone far. Thousands of acres in the East and South have been made unfit for tillage. North Carolina was, a century ago, one of the great agricultural states of the country and one of the wealthiest. To-day as you ride through the South you see everywhere land gullied by torrential rains, red and yellow clay banks exposed where once were fertile fields; and agriculture reduced because its main support has been washed away. Millions of acres, in places to the extent of one-tenth of the entire arable area, have been so injured that no industry and no care can restore them.

Far more ruinous, because universal and continuing in its effects, is the process of soil exhaustion. It is creeping over the land from East to West. The abandoned farms that are now the playthings of the city's rich or the game preserves of patrons of sport bear witness to the melancholy change. New Hampshire, Vermont, Northern New York, show long lists of them. In Western Massachusetts, which once supported a flourishing agriculture, farm properties are now for sale for half the cost of the improvements.

The same process of deterioration is affecting the farm lands of Western New York, Ohio and Indiana. Where prices of farms should rise by increase of population, in many places they are falling. Official investigation of two counties in Central New York disclosed a condition of agricultural decay. In one, land was for sale for about the cost of improvements, and 150 vacant houses were counted in a limited area. In the other, the population in 1905 was nearly 4,000 less than in 1855.

Practically identical soil conditions exist in Maryland and Virginia, where lands sell at from $10 to $30 an acre. In a hearing before an Industrial Commission the chief of the Bureau of Soils of the Department of Agriculture said: "One of the most important causes of deterioration, and I think I should put this first of all, is the method and system of agriculture that prevails throughout these states. Unquestionably the soil has been abused." The richest region of the West is no more exempt than New England or the South. The soil of the West is being reduced in agricultural potency by exactly the same processes which have driven the farmer of the East, with all his advantage of nearness to markets, from the field.

Within the last forty years a great part of the richest land in the country has been brought under cultivation. We should, therefore, in the same time, have raised proportionately the yield of our principal crops per acre, because the yield of old lands, if properly treated, tends to increase rather than diminish. The year 1906 was one of large crops and can scarcely be taken as a standard. We produced, for example, more corn that year than had ever been grown in the United States in a single year before. But the average yield per acre was less than it was in 1872. We are barely keeping the acre product stationary. The average wheat crop of the country now ranges from 12½, in ordinary years, to 15 bushels per acre in the best seasons.

But the fact of soil waste becomes startlingly evident when we examine the record of some states where single cropping and other agricultural abuses have been prevalent. Take the case of wheat, the mainstay of single crop abuse. Many can remember when New York was the great wheat-producing state of the Union. The average yield of wheat per acre in New York for the last ten years was about 18 bushels. For the first five years of that ten-year period it was 18.4 bushels, and for the last five 17.4 bushels. In the farther West, Kansas takes high rank as a wheat producer. Its average yield per acre for the last ten years was 14.16 bushels. For the first five of those years it was 15.14 and for the last five 13.18. Up in the Northwest, Minnesota wheat has made a name all over the world. Her average yield per acre for the same ten years was 12.96 bushels. For the first five years it was 13.12 and for the last five 12.8. We perceive here the working of a uniform law, independent of location, soil or climate. It is the law of a diminishing return due to soil destruction. Apply this to the country at large, and it reduces agriculture to the condition of a bank whose depositors are steadily drawing out more money than they put in.

What is true in this instance is true of our agriculture as a whole. In no other important country in the world, with the exception of Russia, is the industry that must be the foundation of every state at so low an ebb as in our own. According to the last census the average annual product per acre of the farms of the whole United States was worth $11.38. It is little more than a respectable rental in communities where the soil is properly cared for and made to give a reasonable return for cultivation. Nature has given to us the most valuable possession ever committed to man. It can never be duplicated, because there is none like it upon the face of the earth. And we are racking and impoverishing it exactly as we are felling the forests and rifling the mines. Our soil, once the envy of every other country, the attraction which draws millions of immigrants across the seas, gave an average yield for the whole United States during the ten years beginning with 1896 of 13.5 bushels of wheat per acre. Austria and Hungary each produced over 17 bushels per acre, France 19.8, Germany 27.6 and the United Kingdom 32.2 bushels per acre. For the same decade our average yield of oats was less than 30 bushels, while Germany produced 46 and Great Britain 42. For barley the figures are 25 against 33 and 34.6; for rye 15.4 against 24 for Germany and 26 for Ireland. In the United Kingdom, Belgium, The Netherlands and Denmark a yield of more than 30 bushels of wheat per acre has been the average for the past five years.

When the most fertile land in the world produces so much less than that of poorer quality elsewhere, and this low yield shows a tendency to steady decline, the situation becomes clear. We are robbing the soil, in an effort to get the largest cash returns from each acre of ground in the shortest possible time and with the least possible labour. This soil is not mere dead matter, subject to any sort of treatment with impunity. Chemically, it contains elements which must be present in certain proportions for the support of vegetation. Physically, it is made up of matter which supplies the principal plant food. This food, with its chemical constituents in proper admixture, is furnished by the decomposition of organic matter and the disintegration of mineral matter proceeding together. Whatever disturbs either factor of the process, whatever takes out of the soil an excessive amount of one or more of the chemical elements upon which plant growth depends, ends in sterility. Any agricultural methods that move in this direction mean soil impoverishment; present returns at the cost of future loss; the exhaustion of the land exactly as the human system is enfeebled by lack of proper nourishment.

Our agricultural lands have been abused in two principal ways; first, by single cropping, and, second, by neglecting fertilization. It is fortunate for us that nature is slow to anger, and that we may arrest the consequence of this ruinous policy before it is too late.

In all parts of the United States, with only occasional exceptions, the system of tillage has been to select the crop which would bring in most money at the current market rate, to plant that year after year, and to move on to virgin fields as soon as the old farm rebelled by lowering the quality and quantity of its return. It is still the practice, although diversification of industry and the rotation of crops have been urged for nearly a century and are to-day taught in every agricultural college in this country.

The demonstration of the evils of single cropping is mathematical in its completeness. At the experiment station of the Agricultural College of the University of Minnesota they have maintained 44 experimental plots of ground, adjoining one another, and as nearly identical in soil, cultivation and care as scientific handling can make them. On these have been tried and compared different methods of crop rotation and fertilization, together with systems of single cropping. The results of ten years' experiment are available. On a tract of good ground sown continuously for 10 years to wheat, the average yield per acre for the first five years was 20.22 bushels and for the next five 16.92 bushels. Where corn was grown continuously on one plot, while on the plot beside it corn was planted but once in five years in a system of rotation, the average yield of the latter for the two years it was under corn was 48.2 bushels per acre. The plot where corn only was grown gave 20.8 bushels per acre for the first five and 11.1 bushels for the second five of these years, an average of 16 bushels. The difference in average of these two plots was 32.2 bushels, or twice the total yield of the ground exhausted by the single-crop system. The corn grown at the end of the ten years was hardly hip high, the ears small and the grains light. But the cost of cultivation remained the same. And the same is true of every other grain or growth when raised continuously on land unfertilized. We frequently hear it said that the reduction in yield is due to the wearing out of the soil. The fact is that soils either increase or maintain their productivity indefinitely under proper cultivation.

The remedies are as well ascertained as is the evil. Rotation of crops and the use of fertilizers act as tonics upon the soil. The more careful and thorough the tillage, the less the waste and the speedier the restoration of soil values. We might expand our resources and add billions of dollars to our national wealth by conserving soil resources, instead of exhausting them, as we have the forests and the contents of the mines.

Every intelligent and progressive farmer will join stock raising with grain raising. Nature has provided the cattle to go with the land. There is as much money in live stock as there is in grain. Looked at in any way, there is money in live stock; money for dairy products, money for beef, money for the annual increase, and most money of all for the next year's crop when every particle of manure is saved and applied to the land.

We need not consider at present really intensive farming, such as is done by market gardeners with high profit, or such culture as in France, in Holland, in Belgium and in the island of Jersey produces financial returns per acre that seem almost beyond belief. What our people have to do is to cover less ground, cultivate smaller farms so as to make the most of them, instead of getting a scant and uncertain yield from several hundred acres, and raise productivity by intelligent treatment to twice or three times its present level.

There is more money in this system. The net profit from an acre of wheat on run-down soils is very small; consequently decreasing the acreage of wheat under certain conditions will not materially decrease profits. Here are some reliable estimates. The price of wheat is given from the United States Department of Agriculture Yearbook, average for ten years:

YIELD	PRICE	MARKET VALUE PER ACRE	COST OF PRODUCTION INCLUDING RENT	NET PROFIT OR LOSS
20	$0.638	$12.76	$7.89	+$4.87
16	"	10.21	"	+ 2.32
12	"	7.66	"	— 0.23
10	"	6.38	"	— 1.51
8	"	5.10	"	— 2.79

From the above table it will be seen that as large a net profit is realized from one crop of 20 bushels per acre as from two crops of 16 bushels; and that a 12-bushel crop or less yields a net loss. It is a safe conclusion that 75 acres of land, growing a crop of clover every fourth year, will yield a larger net profit than will 100 acres sown to grain continually. A small field of eight acres of clover in the Red River valley in 1907 yielded 42 bushels, worth over $60 per acre from the sale of seed.

Nearly 36 per cent. of our people are engaged directly in agriculture. But all the rest depend upon it. In the last analysis, commerce, manufactures, our home market, every form of activity runs back to the bounty of the earth by which every worker, skilled and unskilled, must be fed and by which his wages are ultimately paid. The farm products of the United States in 1906 were valued at $6,794,000,000 and in 1908 at $7,778,-000,000. All of our vast domestic commerce, equal in value to the foreign trade of all the nations combined, is supported and paid for by the land. Of our farm area only one-half is improved. It does not produce one-half of what it could be made to yield; not by some complex system of intensive culture, but merely by ordinary care and industry intelligently applied. It is the capital upon which alone we can draw through all the future, but the amount of the draft that will be honoured depends upon the care and intelligence given to its cultivation. Nowhere in the range of national purposes is the reward for conservation of a national resource so ample. Nowhere is the penalty of neglect so threatening.

The pressure of all the nations upon the waste places of the earth grows more intense as the last of them are occupied. We are approaching the point where all our wheat product will be needed for our own uses, and we shall cease to be an exporter of grain. There is still some room in Canada, but it will soon be filled. The relief will be but temporary. Our own people, whose mineral resources will by that time have greatly diminished, must find themselves thrown back upon the soil for a living. If continued abuse of the land should mark the next 50 years as it has the last, what must be our outlook?

Even the unintelligent are now coming to understand that we cannot look to our foreign trade for relief from future embarrassment. Our total exports, about one-fourth in value of the products of our farms, and destined to shrink as consumption overtakes production, consist to the extent of more than 70 per cent. of articles grown on the soil or directly sustained by it, such as live stock, or made from soil products, such as flour. Of all the materials used in manufacture in this country, 42 per cent. are furnished by the soil. We shall have less and less of this agricultural wealth to part with as population increases. And as to enlarging greatly our sale of manufactured products in the world's markets, it is mostly a dream. We cannot finally compete there, except in a few selected lines, without a material lowering of the wage scale at home and a change in the national standard of living which our people are not ready to accept without a struggle. When capital cannot find a profit there will be no money for the pay-rolls of an unprofitable business. Doubtless as we grow we shall buy more and sell more; but our main dependence half a century ahead must be upon ourselves. The nation can no more escape the operation of that law than can the man.

Not only the economic, but the political future is involved. No people ever felt the want of work or the pinch of poverty for a long time without reaching out violent hands against their political institutions, believing that they might find in a change some relief from their distress. Although there have been moments of such restlessness in our country, the trial has never been so severe or so prolonged as to put us to the test. It is interesting that one of the ablest men in England during the last century, a historian of high merit, a statesman who saw active service and a profound student of men and things, put on record his prophecy of such a future ordeal. Writing to an American correspondent 50 years ago, Lord Macaulay used these words:

"As long as you have a boundless extent of fertile and unoccupied land your labouring population will be found more at ease than the labouring population of the Old World; but the time will come when wages will be as low and will fluctuate as much with you as they do with us. Then your institutions will be brought to the test. Distress everywhere makes the labourer mutinous and discontented and inclines him to listen with eagerness to agitators who tell him that it is a monstrous iniquity that one man should have a million and another cannot get a full meal. . . . The day will come when the multitudes of people, none of whom has had more than half a breakfast or expects to have more than half a dinner, will choose a legislature. Is it possible to doubt what sort of legislature will be chosen? . . . There will be, I fear, spoliation. The spoliation will increase the distress; the distress will produce fresh spoliation. . . . Either civilization or liberty will perish. Either some Cæsar or Napoleon will seize the reins of government with a strong hand, or your republic will be as fearfully plundered and laid waste by barbarians in the twentieth century as the Roman Empire in the fifth."

We need not accept this gloomy picture too literally, but we have been already sufficiently warned to prevent us from dismissing the subject as unworthy of attention. Every nation finds its hour of peril when there is no longer free access to the land, or when the land will no longer support the people. Disturbances within are more to be feared than attacks from without. Our government is built upon the assumption of a fairly contented, prosperous and happy people, capable of ruling their passions, with power to change their institutions when such change is generally desired. It would not be strange if they should in their desire for change attempt to pull down the pillars of their national temple. Far may this day be from us. But since the unnecessary destruction of our land will bring new conditions of danger, its conservation, its improvement to the highest point of productivity promised by scientific intelligence and practical experiment, appears to be a first command of any political economy worthy of the name.

These are for us quite literally the issues of national

existence. The era of unlimited expansion on every side, of having but to reach out and seize any desired good, ready provided for us by the Hand that laid the foundations of the earth, is drawing to a close. The first task is to force the facts of the situation deep into the public consciousness; to make men realize their duty toward coming generations exactly as the father feels it a duty to see that his children do not suffer want. In a democracy this is a first essential. In other forms of government one or two great men may have power to correct mistakes and to put in motion wise policies that centuries do not unsettle. A part of the price of self-government is the acceptance of that high office and imperative duty as a whole by the people themselves. They must know, they must weigh, they must act. Only as they form and give effect to wise decisions can the nation go forward. The principle of the conservation of national resources as the foremost and controlling policy of the United States henceforth is coming to be seen by many, and must be heartily accepted by all, as the first condition, not only of continued material prosperity, but also of the perpetuation of free institutions and a government by the people. The work now being done by the Department of Agriculture and the agricultural colleges of the various states furnishes a broad and intelligent foundation upon which to build up a new era of national progress and prosperity. It calls for a wise, generous and continuing policy on the part of both federal and state governments.

If this patriotic gospel is to make headway, it must

be by organized missionary work among the people, and by the people. It cannot go on and conquer if imposed from without. It must come to represent the fixed idea of the people's mind, their determination and their hope. It cannot be incorporated in our practical life by the dictum of any individual or any officer of nation or state in his official capacity. It needs the coöperation of all the influences, the help of every voice, the commendation of nation and state that has been the strength and inspiration of every worthy work on American soil for one hundred and twenty years. Reviving thus the spirit of the days that created our Constitution, the days that carried us through civil conflict, the spirit by which all our enduring work in the world has been wrought, taking thought as Washington and Lincoln took thought, only for the highest good of all the people, we may give new meaning to our future; new lustre to the ideal of a republic of living federated states; shape anew the fortunes of this country, and enlarge the borders of hope for all mankind.

THE END

INDEX

INDEX

ABANDONED FARMS: (See Farm)

ACREAGE: Cultivated, 37; uncultivated, 37; wheat, 73, 74

AFRICA, DARKEST: 109

AGRICULTURE: (See Chaps. I, II, III, XVI, also Farming) area, 7, 198; American, 19, 20, 76; and drainage (See Drainage), 194; and irrigation (See Irrigation); and natural wealth, 54, 154; Department of, 33, 77, 316, 322, 327; essentials of, 31, 81; experiments in, 32, 35, 320; exports (See Exports); importance of, 15, 23, 40, 42, 45, 46, 47, 63, 84; improvement, 41, 59, 73, 80; in Belgium, 30, 31; in Denmark, 82, 83; in 1850 and in 1900, 143; in France, 29, 30; in Germany, 27, 28, 76; in Great Britain, 26, 27, 75; in Japan, 28, 51; in Jersey, island of, 30; in Netherlands, 83; in Northwest, 143, 144; in United States, 16, 23, 24, 36, 315, 316, 317, 318, 319, 320, 321, 322, 323; intensive (See Farming); labour (See also Labour), 40, 55, 167; modern methods, 80, 81, 154; possibilities of, 30, 31, 32, 33, 34, 35, 36, 37, 72, 82, 198, 200

AGRICULTURAL COLLEGES: 60, 61, 73, 320

AGRICULTURAL EDUCATION: 58, 59, 61, 62

AGRICULTURAL POPULATION: (See Population)

AGRICULTURAL WEALTH: Increase, 20, 25, 36, 82, 201, 205, 221, 239, 282, 322; in France, 29; in United States, 20, 25, 43, 322

ALABAMA: 165

ALASKA: 204, 314

ALBERTA: 191

ALEXANDER THE GREAT, 158

ALLEGHANIES: 235

AMERICAN CHARACTERISTICS: (See Traits)

AMERICAN COLONIES: 88

AMERICAN DESERT: 198

ANNALS OF THE AMERICAN ACADEMY: 97

ANTI-TRUST LAW: (See Sherman Law)

ANTWERP: 168, 214

APPROPRIATIONS: 225, 228, 229, 293, 295, 332

AREA, UNITED STATES: compared with Europe, 52; cultivated, 25, 37; uncultivated, 25, 37

ARGENTINA: 106

HIGHWAYS OF PROGRESS 335

271, 273, 281; distance tariff, 281, European, 212, 214; export, 166, 167, 171, 172, 173; freight per mile, 240, 262; high, 255; how fixed, 252, 254, 258; in Austria, 262; in Europe, 262; in France, 262; in Germany, 213, 262; in Great Britain, 261, 262; in Hesse, 214; increase, 254, 263, 264, 281; just, 255, 264; lake and rail, 147, 215, 216, 218; local, 173; low, 150, 163, 171, 173, 254, 255, 256, 257, 258, 262, 263, 283, 299; lumber, 159, 163, 257; maximum and minimum, 173, 254, 258; merchandise, 257; notice of change, 172; New York and Chicago, 215; ocean (See Ocean Rates); passenger per mile, 240, 261, 262, 272; principles of, 254, 255, 256, 259; Prussian, 214; published, 173; reasonable, 128, 133, 254, 256, 258, 259, 260, 264, 267, 284; reduction in United States, 127, 130, 150, 210, 260, 272, 280; regulation (See also Interstate Commerce Commission), 129, 172, 173; revenue, 240; special, 273; standard, 282; transcontinental, 163; United States, 214; unreasonable, 128; volume of business, 159, 253, 254; wars, 126, 258; wheat, 150, 215, 256, 257.

RAILROADS: (See Chaps. VI, XII, XIII, XIV); (For separate systems see Great Northern, etc.) 120; abuse of, 283, 284; additions, 241, 247, 248; age, 204; and

capital, 247, 248; and drainage, 187, 206, 207; and farmer, 135, 153, 206, 255, 256; and irrigation, 21, 189, 190, 206, 207; and trade, 108, 238; and waterways (See Waterways); betterments, 150, 151, 248, 252, 266; Bureau of News and Statistics, 251, 261, 262; business enterprise, 135, 153; capacity, 241; capitalization (See Railroad Capitalization); car service, 245, 246, 247; cars, freight, 240, 243, 272; car shortage, 247; cars, passenger, 240; congestion, 240, 241, 243, 244; consolidation (See also Chap. VI), 129, 133, 134, 237, 238; construction (See also Chap. XII), 237; control (See Railroad Legislation); controversy, 250; cost (See also Railroad Capitalization), 266, 283; cost of operation, 238, 247, 272; cost of service, 256, 258, 259, 263, 273; creators, 236, 282; damage suits, 276; density of traffic (See Traffic); depreciation, 252; distribution of gross earnings, 266; dividends (See also Chap. XIII), 248, 252; early, 125, 209, 236, 237; economies, 129, 238, 261, 272; efficiency, 127, 130, 133, 238, 242, 243, 244, 245, 247, 272, 275; employees, 263, 274, 282; equipment, 240, 241, 242, 243, 246; evolution (See Evolution); expenses, 273, 277; facilities, 236; failure, 283; finances (See also Chap. XIII), 126, 248, 249; first, 235; freight

Why Businessmen Need a Philosophy of Capitalism

Capitalism has built the modern world. Although there are some who would dispute that claim, it is clear, at least for those who examine the facts without bias or political intent, that economies based on capitalism are stronger and expand at a faster rate than other economic systems. This fact has been well established throughout history.

At its simplest and purest, capitalism is an economic system in which private individuals and companies produce and exchange goods and services through free markets. Ideally, capitalism is not hindered by governmental controls; in reality, however, there are many shades and nuances of capitalism that result in economic systems that are often described as a *mixed economy*. In some lands, capitalism is restrained by laws and governmental regulations; the degree determined by political and social objectives. Many political leaders hope to influence their people via the economy, they may attempt to protect domestic business from foreign competition, or they may try to increase revenue with tariffs or export duties. That these types of objectives usually only hinder economic activity over the long term is frequently ignored, lost in the rhetoric about social considerations and goals.

Of the many factors that can affect how the capitalist spirit develops in a country, one which is often overlooked is that of entrepreneurship. In lands where capitalism is unfettered by unnecessary regulation and where entrepreneurship is dynamic, impressive economic gains and advancements can be expected. Entrepreneurship is perhaps one of the greatest driving forces of capitalism. Indeed, the two are inseparable.

Capitalism is an economic system in which the means of production and distribution are privately owned and operated, and an entrepreneur is an individual who undertakes to start and conduct a business. Entrepreneurs propel capitalism forward. The bottom line here is quite clear: if a person is restricted in his ownership of a business through governmental regulations or social constraints, why should he or she risk starting any economic enterprise? Conversely, if an individual perceives that his or her efforts will be the overall deciding factor in economic gain or loss, he or she is more likely to risk investment in a business venture.

The world has seen many different economic systems throughout history. With its origins deep in the mists of ancient societies, barter was one of the first economies in which individuals and groups exchanged goods and services, paying for one commodity with another. Rudimentary forms of capitalism were not far behind and their origins are likewise obscure. Capitalism is generally thought to have arisen in various places around the world, gained prominence in old Europe centuries ago where it developed slowly and gradually spread through most of the world, reaching its zenith during the 19th century and remaining dominant until World War I. For a time during the 20th century, communism, a system in which the state plays a major role in economic ownership, regulation, and intervention, challenged capitalism's dominance, particularly in the Eastern Hemisphere, but as the century ended, capitalism, in one form of another, has re-emerged as the world's premier economic system.

The effect of capitalism extends far beyond economics, however, for capitalism is a major factor in the evolution of nations. Virtually every great nation through history has been a potent economic power as well. An excellent example of this in the 20th century is the ascendance of the Soviet Union as a world power after World War II. For a time the Soviet Union, founded on communism, seemed ready to challenge the United States for world military, cultural, and economic supremacy, but their threat was short-lived. While some observers of the world scene argue that it was American President Ronald Reagan's hard-line military stance against the Soviet Union that led to the eventual breakup and dissolution of that communist state, it was American economic power, based on capitalism, that provided Reagan with the foundation on which he could make his stand. Communism could not keep pace with America's economic strength. Reagan's policies also have led to the People's Republic of China slowly but steadily turning to capitalism to enhance their economy. Mainland China's appreciation of capitalism is well illustrated with the reversion of Hong Kong – one of the world's greatest free-market success stories – to Mainland control and the pledge of the Chinese government not to tamper with Hong Kong's economy, a promise the Chinese have honored.

The resurgence of capitalism at the end of the 20th century has been driven by a powerful tide of entrepreneurship in the technology sector, most apparent in the explosive growth of the Internet, and has led to spectacular economic gains. E-commerce (electronic commerce) is without question changing the way the world does business, and it can easily be termed E-capitalism.

We are in a period in which economic opportunity has seldom been greater. As technology and the Internet continue to advance, every business or enterprise that can benefit from them has the opportunity to advance as well. Ten years ago, few of the top Internet companies had even been imagined. Ten years ago, we were only on the verge of the new capitalist economy that, while built on the old principles of capitalism, is immeasurably enhanced by technological know-how. Ten years ago, traditional businesses were still the norm. And now, new ideas are giving rise to new companies every day. The businesses, services, and companies that may dominate the economic landscape ten years from now are still in the formulation stages of their creators. The opportunities for entrepreneurs are perhaps greater than ever.

Certainly we are witnessing the coming of a new economic age in which those individuals and companies that produce the goods and services that satisfy the needs of a modern, fast-paced world will be the most successful. Technology permits customers to buy the items or services they desire with a mere click of a mouse. Individuals who embrace the spirit of the entrepreneur and who are able to ascertain the needs of potential customers stand to benefit handsomely.

After all, entrepreneurs have been creating and running businesses since primitive times. Going back to the earliest societies, farmers, fisherman, and merchants traded their goods and services. Every business that exists today at one time was the dream and ambition of an entrepreneur. The entrepreneur is the visionary, the man or woman with the better idea, the innovator, the doer. It is the entrepreneur who creates the original product, acquires the facilities and materials, obtains the capital, assembles the workforce, and brings the finished product to market. It is also the entrepreneur who reaps the profits of a successful venture. In the case of failure, the entrepreneur stands to take the major loss.

Capitalism and entrepreneurship are closely linked. Capitalism is the economic system most conducive to entrepreneurship, and entrepreneurship provides the innovation and energy of capitalism. Each sustains and gains strength from the other, together forming a solid bedrock for economic activity.

While opportunity for entrepreneurs is present in the most advanced economies, clearly developing economies offer the greatest opportunities because of their nature, which usually includes a rapidly growing middle class with a strong desire for consumer products. As companies attempt to meet the needs of these new consumers, entrepreneurs are likely to find countless opportunities. In advanced nations new products and services are typically brought to market by major corporations that maintain huge staffs, whose primary purpose is the design and creation of new products. In smaller, developing nations, however, niche markets and special needs present an environment that is ripe for innovation. In many of these nations, governments may actively support entrepreneurs through a variety of special programs, including tax incentives, special trade status, and an assortment of grants, to encourage investment and economic activity. The leaders of such governments are aware that entrepreneurs energize capitalism, which in turn leads to economic growth.

As the global economy continues to expand, world trade will undoubtedly increase. At the same time, because of the growing role of technology, boundaries between nations and markets will shrink, providing entrepreneurs will marvelous opportunities, limited only by their own imaginations. The world is entering a rare and wonderful environment for the entrepreneur.

An extensive library of articles on capitalism and free-markets is at http://www.libertyhaven.com

Afterword by Adam Starchild

Over the past 25 years, Adam Starchild has been the author of over two dozen books, and hundreds of magazine articles, primarily on business and finance. His articles have appeared in a wide range of publications around the world — including Business Credit, Euromoney, Finance, The Financial Planner, International Living, Offshore Financial Review, Reason, Tax Planning International, The Bull & Bear, Trust & Estates, and many more.

Now semi-retired, he was the president of an international consulting group specializing in banking, finance and the development of new businesses, and director of a trust company.

Although this formidable testimony to expertise in his field, plus his current preoccupation with other books-in-progress, would not seem to leave time for a well-rounded existence, Starchild has won two Presidential Sports Awards and written several cookbooks, and is currently involved in a number of personal charitable projects.

His personal website is at http://www.cyberhaven.com/starchild/